Volume 2: Essential Modeling Techniques

Structured Development for Real-Time Systems

D1558562

YOURDON COMPUTING SERIES
Ed Yourdon, *Advisor*

Volume 2: Essential Modeling Techniques

Structured Development for Real-Time Systems

by Paul T. Ward &
Stephen J. Mellor

YOURDON PRESS
A Prentice-Hall Company
Englewood Cliffs, New Jersey 07632

Library of Congress Catalog Number 85-50815

Printed in the United States of America

10   9   8   7   6

ISBN   0-13-854795-5   025

Prentice-Hall International (UK) Limited, *London*
Prentice-Hall of Australia Pty. Limited, *Sydney*
Prentice-Hall Canada Inc., *Toronto*
Prentice-Hall Hispanoamericana, S.A., *Mexico*
Prentice-Hall of India Private Limited, *New Delhi*
Prentice-Hall of Japan, Inc., *Tokyo*
Prentice-Hall of Southeast Asia Pte. Ltd., *Singapore*
Editora Prentice-Hall do Brasil, Ltda., *Rio de Janeiro*

Dedications

To Pamela with Love

— P.T.W.

To both my families

— S.J.M.

ACKNOWLEDGMENTS

We stated our gratefulness to various colleagues for contributions to the genesis of our approach in the Acknowledgments for Volume 1, and we wish to reiterate our gratefulness here.

We would particularly like to thank the technical reviewers of Volume 2 for their hard work and for their helpful insights: Pete Coad, Jr., Charles S. Hendrickson, Peter J. Gross, Steven Weiss, and W.K. Krutz.

A special word of thanks is due to John Shuttleworth of N.V. Philips. John was the author of the original version of the SILLY case study, and generously permitted us to include a version of the case study in this volume.

Finally, we wish to express our gratitude to Gerry Madigan and the Yourdon Press editorial staff.

CONTENTS

Preface

Over the last forty-odd years, builders of automated systems have learned, often at great expense, that a rigorous notation alone does not assure a satisfactory product. Without the discipline of structured programming and other facets of programming style, the use of even the most elegant language can degenerate into ill-organized "hacking."

The rules of structured programming are of a different character from the syntax rules of a programming language. The latter admit no exceptions; the former are more properly guidelines or heuristics than rules, and do admit exceptions. (There are, of course, always zealots ready and willing to turn guidelines into rigid rules. We refer the reader to the interminable literature on the "goto" controversy for examples.)

The subject of this volume bears the same relationship to the modeling notation set out in Volume 1 as structured programming bears to programming language syntax. We have attempted to synthesize the experiences of many developers on many systems into a "style" for modeling requirements. Our experience indicates that the combination of modeling tools and modeling heuristics presented in these two volumes provides an effective approach to real-time systems development. We hope our readers will have the same experience.

Introduction to
Essential Modeling Heuristics Section

In this section — comprising the whole of volume 2 — the modeling tools introduced in section 2 of Volume 1 are applied to the building of an essential model.

Chapter 1, Essential Modeling Heuristics, explains the overall guidelines for essential model building that recur in various ways in the remaining chapters.

Chapters 2 and 3 form a unit concerned with modeling a system's environment. Chapter 2, Defining System Context, focuses on the representation of system scope. Chapter 3, Modeling External Events, examines the identification of the stimuli to which a system must respond.

Chapters 4, 5 and 6 also form a unit, this time concerned with modeling a system's behavior once the environment has been established. Chapter 4, Deriving the Behavioral Model, describes the translation of an event list into a schematic model. Chapter 5, Completing the Essential Model — the Upper Levels, introduces guidelines for reorganizing the initial schematic model for presentation. Chapter 6, Completing the Essential Model — the Lower Levels, describes methods for incorporating lower-level details into the model.

Finally, Chapter 7, Essential Model Traceability, describes the keeping of detailed records documenting the derivation of the essential model.

Because of the subject matter of this section, the examples are of necessity more elaborate than those in Section 2 of Volume 1. To avoid incorporating large amounts of background material on the examples in the chapters themselves, we have chosen nearly all the examples from the same four systems. The background descriptions for these systems, together with fully-worked-out essential models, are to be found in Appendices A, B, C, and D.

The reader is urged first to read the background material, then to read the chapters, and finally to examine the essential models in detail.

NOTE ON PRELIMINARY EDITION

We are publishing this preliminary edition in three volumes. The first volume serves as an introduction and describes a set of general tools for modeling the complexities of real-time systems. The second volume addresses the techniques of essential modeling (loosely, systems analysis). It shows how the tools are used to construct a model of what needs to be done. The third volume addresses the techniques of implementation modeling (loosely, systems design). These techniques use the tools described in the introductory volume plus some additional tools to construct a model of the chosen solution.

We are eagerly seeking feedback from our professional colleagues on improvements in presentation and content. We intend to incorporate this feedback into a subsequent edition of this book to be published in the near future.

1
Essential Modeling Heuristics

1.1 Introduction

In *Structured Development for Real-Time Systems*, Volume 1, Chapter 4 (Modeling Heuristics), we defined an essential model as one that describes those things that a system must do to be successful, regardless of the technology chosen to implement it. In Chapters 6 through 13 of Volume 1, we introduced a modeling notation, which, as we shall demonstrate, is adequate to express the details of an essential model rigorously.

Unfortunately, neither an understanding of the characteristics of an essential model, nor a knowledge of the modeling notation, guarantees that a successful model can actually be built. Some guidelines — some modeling heuristics — are needed. These heuristics must be specific enough to provide detailed guidance to the model-builder yet general enough to cover the spectrum of situations in which an essential model must be built.

In this chapter we will introduce three powerful guidelines for essential model building: environment-based modeling, subject-matter-centered modeling, and minimum-complexity representation. Before discussing these in detail, let's look at a commonly used heuristic for modeling requirements and examine its inadequacies.

1.2 Problems with functional decomposition

Functional decomposition is a specific application of the idea of top-down development discussed in Volume 1, Chapter 4. The developer begins by envisioning a system, or part of a system, as a single function (in other words, as a transformation of inputs into outputs). The system is then decomposed into a small set of subfunctions equivalent to the original function, and the interfaces between the subfunctions are identified. Each subfunction then becomes the starting point for a further decomposition into sub-subfunctions and identification of lower-level interfaces. The process continues until the lowest level of functions is simple enough to be specified in detail.

As an example, consider the specification of a control system for a picture-taking satellite. The modeler using functional decomposition might conceive of the overall function of the system as "Manage optical data collection." This function might then be decomposed into "Manage data transmission," "Manage data storage," "Manage mechanical equipment control," and other major subfunctions. "Manage data transmission" might be further decomposed into "Manage message input" and "Manage message output," and so on. Figure 1.1 illustrates this process schematically.

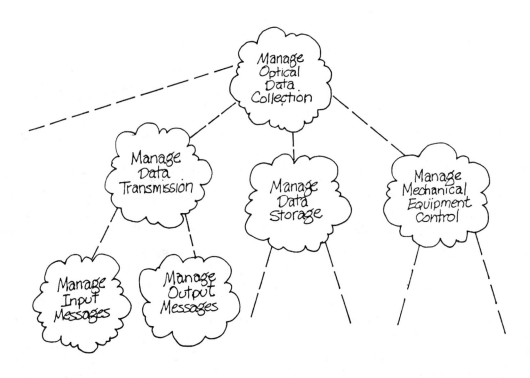

Figure 1.1 Illustration of functional decomposition.

Functional decomposition has an attractive pedigree: it was one of the earliest development techniques, and it neatly matches top-down *presentation* techniques such as the notation described in Chapter 12 of Volume 1 (Organizing the Model). Nevertheless, there are major problems with this approach. First, Heitmeyer and McLean [1] argue that any statement of requirements arrived at by decomposition is implementation-dependent, since a more-or-less arbitrary choice among a set of possible decompositions has been made. An arbitrary choice of subsystems boundaries imposed by decomposition may thus prevent an implementer from using perfectly adequate algorithms that happen to be inconsistent with these boundaries.

Second, it has been our experience that the technique often does not produce good partitionings. Although criteria exist for evaluating alternate decompositions on the basis of interface complexity (Parnas [2] and DeMarco [3]), this is an after-the-fact approach that eliminates possible solutions only after the work is put in to create them. Functional decomposition does nothing to *guide* the developer to a partitioning with minimum interfaces. The technique thus invites "analysis paralysis," in which endless discussions of the merits of various top-level partitionings of the model preclude progress toward understanding of the specifics.

These problems, taken together, cause us to regard functional decomposition as being of very limited value.

We feel that the shortcomings of functional decomposition arise from its failure to make explicit use of all the information available to the developer at requirements definition. Specifically, functional decomposition fails to focus on the environment in which the system to be built must operate.

This leads to our next topic, the application of environment-based modeling to the building of an essential model.

1.3 Environment-based modeling

To be sure that all the relevant information about the environment is captured in the essential model, it is beneficial actually to *incorporate* a model of the environment into the essential model. Modeling the environment provides a framework that is an alternative to functional decomposition.

The most important task in developing the environmental model is to specify the events to which the system must respond. This specification is the basis for the creation of a behavioral model, using an elaboration of a technique developed by McMenamin and Palmer [4].

Let's recall the picture-taking satellite example used to illustrate functional decomposition. Instead of attempting to identify subfunctions, sub-subfunctions, and so on, environment-based modeling would proceed by identifying events that require some system response. Possible events are "Line of sight of camera is aligned with target" and "Picture-taking request is made." The behavioral model is then constructed by determining acceptable responses to the events, as illustrated in Figure 1.2.

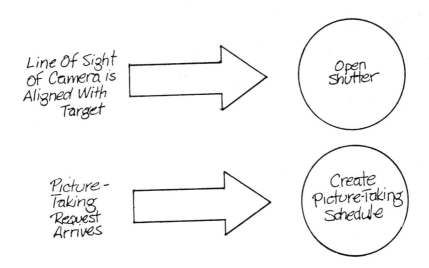

Figure 1.2 Illustration of environment-based modeling.

Although the behavioral model is a functional model (that is, it consists of a collection of transformations of inputs into outputs), it is derived not through decomposition but by a *mapping* of elements from the system's environment into the model. Like the result of functional decomposition, the behavioral model can be represented by a leveled set of transformation schemas. In this case, the event responses would be aggregated into higher-level subsystems.

The event modeler carries out the mapping between the environmental and behavioral models by thinking of a system as a stimulus-response mechanism, which accomplishes a specific purpose by responding to events that occur in its environment. The identification of the events — the elemental stimuli that elicit a response from the system — provides a natural level of detail for a system description. The behavioral model has a point-by-point correspondence to identifiable parts of the environment in which the system will operate. It therefore has a low-level structure derived directly from the structure of the problem and should not bias the developer toward non-optimal solutions. In contrast to functional decomposition, this procedure may be thought of as "outside-in" rather than "top-down" modeling.

Although focusing on the system environment is useful, not all environmental elements are of equal relevance. Before examining the second major essential-modeling heuristic, subject-matter-centered modeling, let's look at a classification scheme for these elements.

1.4 Components of the total system

We focus in this book on systems that will ultimately involve building or adapting computer hardware and software to do the work described by the model. Systems of this type used in manufacturing, aerospace, and similar technological environments are called *embedded systems*. They are part of, and contribute to, systems that employ technology other than computer technology and whose primary purpose is not computation. An air traffic control system, for example, contains radars, radio transmitters, and radio receivers in addition to computers. Its purpose is to get aircraft safely into and out of some defined airspace: The computations performed by the computers within such a system, while important, are completely subordinate to the purpose of the larger system.

Alford [5] has proposed a characterization of the larger systems of which embedded systems are a part. Such systems have a *perception space* and an *action space* as illustrated by Figure 1.3. *Objects* (vehicles, people, and so on) enter the perception space of the system, are perceived by it, are acted upon, and finally leave the action space of the system. Some examples are given in Table 1.1

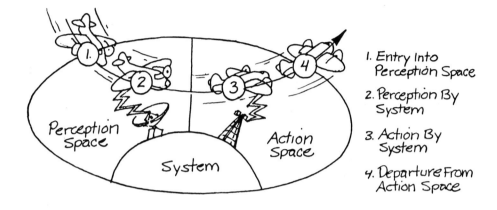

1. Entry Into
   Perception Space

2. Perception By
   System

3. Action By
   System

4. Departure From
   Action Space

Figure 1.3 Perception-action view of an air traffic control system.

System	Entry Into Perception Space	Perception By System	Action By System	Exit From Action Space
Air Traffic Control	Aircraft Flies Into Airspace	Radar spots plane	Course Change Request Radioed To Plane.	Aircraft Flies Out of Airspace
Manufacturing	Raw Materials Physically Enter Plant	Raw Materials Are Incorporated Into Inventory Stores.	Raw Materials Are Transformed Into Finished Items.	Finished Items Leave Plant.
Satellite Surveillance	Location On Earths Surface Comes Into Range.	Photograph Is Taken.	N/A	Location Moves Out of Range.

Table 1.1.

This characterization can easily be extended to traditional business systems: a savings account customer enters a bank, is identified by account number, is given some amount of money from his or her account, and leaves the bank.

In addition to the perception/action space objects, Alford identifies five components of systems matching his characterization: sensors, actors, computers, communication links, and people. We will use a slightly different scheme, lumping people and computers together and identifying the components as sensors, actors, communication links, and processors. (A single device sometimes serves as both a sensor and an actor.) To continue with the air traffic control example, the sensors would be the radar units, the actors would be the equipment that transmitted messages to the aircraft crew, and the communications links would be the data transmission lines, display terminals, and other equipment that passes information and control among radars, transmitters, computers, and air traffic control staff.

Let's now use this classification to describe the application of subject-matter-centered modeling.

1.5 Subject-matter-centered modeling

Consider the components of the total system grouped and listed as perception/action space objects, sensors/actors, communication links, and processors. An ordering has been defined from maximum to minimum subject-matter constraint. The perception/action space objects are, by definition, completely constrained by the subject matter. Changing the nature of these objects changes the nature of the system. A system that perceives and acts on parts on an assembly line has quite a different subject matter from one that perceives and acts on bank customers. Sensors and actors are somewhat constrained by the system's subject matter, but typically have some flexibility in their selection. A satellite cannot use a thermocouple or a pH sensor to detect troop movements on the ground, but it can use any of a wide variety of electromagnetic radiation sensors. Communications links are in turn somewhat constrained by the nature of the sensors and actors that they tie to the system's processors, but the subject-matter-specificity is considerably less. Processors, of course, are by definition subject-matter non-specific, and are thus at the low end of the constraint scale.

The significance of the constraint scale is that only the portions of the (actual or anticipated) environment that are subject-matter-specific should influence the structure of the behavioral model. Let's use as an example the type of keyboard illustrated in Figure 1.4. Depression of a key causes contact between one of the input (read) lines and one of the output (write) lines. The keyboard is operated by periodically energizing the write lines one at a time, then checking the read lines for non-zero voltage. For example, a non-zero voltage on read line 2 while write line 0 is energized means that the '7' key is being depressed.

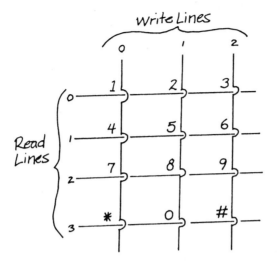

Figure 1.4 Keyboard configuration.

Consider an embedded system that will act as a keyboard device handler. The keyboard is an object in the perception/action space of this system. The values of the read lines are perceived, and the write lines are acted on. It is reasonable to expect functions within the essential model for this device handler to have names drawn from the perception/action space, such as "Energize write line" and "Store read line value."

Now consider a system that operates in a chemical plant to monitor the parameters of a chemical reaction. A system of this kind could be implemented so that a technician reads a dial on the reaction vessel and keys in the reading. Although the keyboard of Figure 1.4 might be used in this system, it plays the role of a *communications link* rather than of a perception/action space object. An essential model for this type of system would contain functions like "Record pH value," referring to the chemical reaction that is the perception/action space object, but should not contain functions referring to the keyboard technology. An implementation change for this system, such as replacing the keyboard by a direct link to the reaction vessel, should not affect the essential model.

1.6 Minimum-complexity representation

Since any system must respond to its environment, the behavioral model of the system must contain some *representation* of the relevant portions of the environment. In the case of an air-traffic control system, one can ask about the system's representation of an aircraft, of the boundaries of the air space, and so on.

The heuristic of minimum-complexity representation states that the simplest representation that adequately models a situation should be chosen. Traditional process-oriented models of business systems have represented the system environment in terms of values of stored data elements. The data transformations in Figure

1.5, for example, are organized around the Inventory Items store. Each entry within the store represents one of the inventory items in the system's environment, including the Quantity Available and the Item ID. The system is represented entirely in terms of data transformations, data flows, and data stores, which is inevitable since these are the only notational elements available in the traditional process model. However, it is reasonable to ask whether the extended notation of the transformation schema is useful for describing this system.

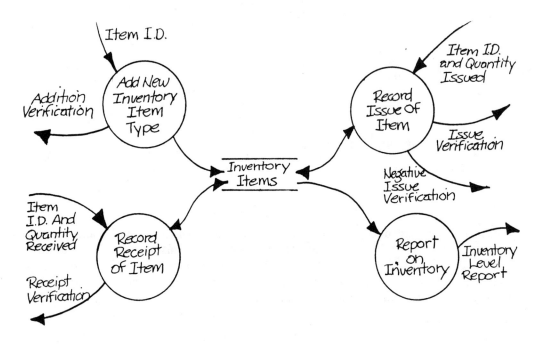

Figure 1.5 Representing the environment in stored data.

To explore this, let's look at a state-transition diagram for a particular inventory item (Figure 1.6). The item isn't in a defined state until it has been added to the system; thereafter it moves between Out of Stock and Available, depending on the pattern of receipts and issues. One could represent the system from Figure 1.5 by incorporating a set of control transformations, one for each existing type of item, each with an associated state diagram identical to Figure 1.6. Each control transformation would manage its own Record Receipt of Item and Record Issue of Item data transformations. The resulting transformation schema is shown in Figure 1.7. Although the notation is quite different, Figure 1.7 has many conceptual similarities to the Jackson System Design method. Jackson and Cameron [6] routinely represent multiple instances of objects in the system's environment by multiple transformations, which they call sequential processes. Each instance of the transformation remembers the status of a particular instance of the object in the system's environment. The specification for the transformation must define the possible values for the status of the object and the permissible sequences of statuses. Contrast this representation to that shown in Figure 1.5. In this model, data about multiple instances of an object in the environment may exist in the store, and the change in status from Available to Out of Stock is managed jointly by Record Receipt of Item and Record Issue of Item.

The coordination required between these two transformations requires only shared data access and is simpler than the stored data and control connections illustrated in Figure 1.7. We therefore argue that Figure 1.5 is preferable because of its simplicity and clarity.

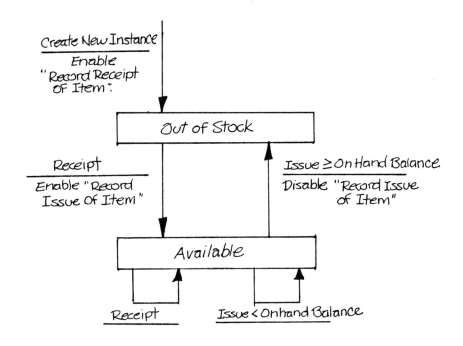

Figure 1.6 State transition diagram for inventory data.

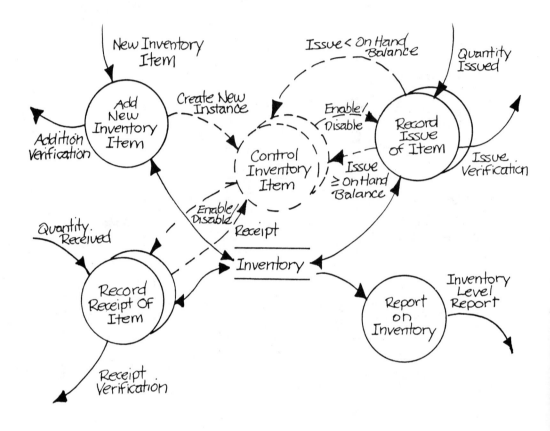

Figure 1.7 Inventory system with control transformations.

Let's now turn the situation around and ask whether situations that we have been modeling with control transformations can be represented more simply in data transformation terms. Figure 1.8 illustrates a model of the Cruise Control System (Appendix A) in which each input is handled by a separate data transformation as was done in Figure 1.5, and in which the Status data store links the transformations and represents the state of the speed control mechanism. The possible values of status are Stopped, Maintaining Speed, Interrupted by Braking, and Resuming Speed. This picture has an appealing simplicity. Unfortunately, the Status data store does not show a true time-delayed connection among the processes as does the Inventory Items store in Figure 1.5. In fact, any change of status will *immediately* impact the behavior of Control Throttle. The model doesn't clearly describe the causal connections between the inputs and the resulting behaviors of the system. Although simple, the representation is not adequate.

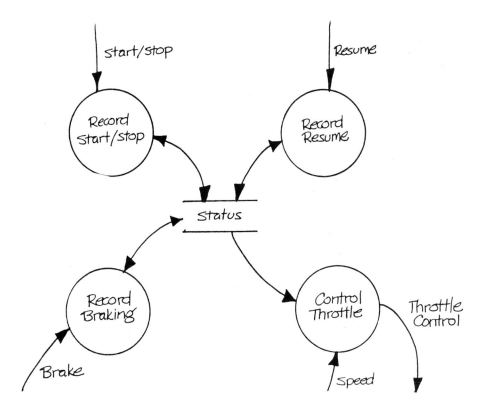

Figure 1.8 Data-transformation-only version of cruise control.

In Figure 1.9, we have used a control transformation to model the interaction between the event flows and the operation of the data transformations. The state transition diagram associated with the Control Speed Maintenance transformation specifies the interaction in discrete terms.

To summarize, one can represent something in a system's environment (sensor/actor technology, or objects in the perception/action space) in either stored data or state transition terms. The stored data representation is characterized by separate data transformations assigned to separate inputs. Connections among transformations are non-causal, time-delayed storage links. The state of the object in the environment is expressed by stored data values. Multiple instances of the object in the environment are expressed by tags, identifying the instance, attached to input flows and to the stored data.

The state transition representation is characterized by a control transformation accepting multiple control inputs and driving multiple data transformations. Connections between transformations are immediate, causal event flow linkages. The state of the object in the environment is represented by a state associated with the control transformation. Multiple instances of the object in the environment are represented by multiple control transformations (multiple sets of states), each controlling individual sets of data transformations. The principle of minimum-complexity representation guides the choice of which representation to use in a particular case.

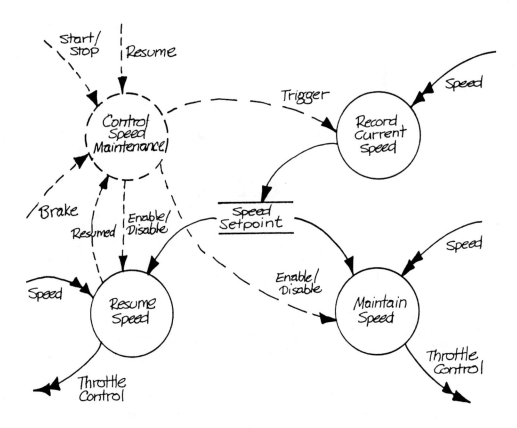

Figure 1.9 Control transformation added to cruise control schema.

1.7 Summary

Essential modeling is fundamentally concerned with the issue of the subject matter of the system and deliberately defers implementation issues. In this chapter we have laid out heuristics for essential modeling that focus on the environment as a basis for constructing a model of the behavior of a system. To clarify the influence of the environment on an embedded system we have identified the roles played by the components of the total system in relation to their roles in an embedded system. Finally, we discussed two ways in which portions of the system can be represented in the essential model and conditions under which each can be the simplest representation of a system's requirements.

Chapter 1 : References

1. C.L. Heitmeyer and J.D. McLean, "Abstract Requirements Specification: A New Approach and Its Application," *IEEE Transactions on Software Engineering,* Volume SE-9. No. 5, Sept. 1983, pp. 580-589.

2 D. Parnas, "On the Criteria to Be Used in Decomposing Systems into Modules." *Communications of the ACM,* Vol. 5, No. 12 (December 1972), pp. 1053-58.

3 T. DeMarco, *Structured Analysis and System Specification.* New York: Yourdon Press, 1978.

4. S. McMenamin and J. Palmer, *Essential Systems Analysis.* New York: Yourdon Press, 1984.

5. M.W. Alford. "An Integrated Data/Control Flow Specification Technique" Paper Presented at the Rocky Mountain Institute for Software Engineering, Aspen, July 1984.

6. M. Jackson and J. Cameron, *A Tutorial on JSD.* London: Michael Jackson Associates, 1984.

2
Defining System Context

2.1 Introduction

It is impossible to create a rigorous system model without a precise and formal delineation of the system's boundaries. We use the term *context* to describe a boundary definition that includes both the interactions between the system and its environment and the things in the environment with which the system interacts. Defining the system context early is crucial to the effective management of a system's life-cycle. Omitting this step is an open invitation to uncoordinated and inefficient development, since there is no verified agreement between developers and sponsors on the scope of what is to be built.

Context definition must be done carefully in order to ensure its usefulness. We consider both the context schema, which will be described in this chapter, and its associated lower-level details as parts of the essential (implementation-independent) system model. Therefore, we need to explore how implementation independence will affect our view of the system in its environment. Furthermore, since some consideration of the system's context must precede any investigation of its function, a context definition should be constructed as an aid in furthering the modeling process.

2.2 Notation for context definition

The notation for representing system context is illustrated in Figure 2.1. The context schema uses an extension of the transformation schema notation; each box represents a *terminator* — something outside the system boundary with which the system interacts — and the transformation, flow, and store symbols are defined as in the transformation schema illustrated in Chapter 6 of Volume 1. The context schema is governed by a number of conventions:

- First, only one transformation representing the entire activity of the system appears on the context diagram.

- Second, only flows that cross the system boundary may appear on the diagram; flows internal to the system are not shown.

- Third, single terminators are used to represent sets of things with which a system interacts. For instance, the terminator Bottle-Filling Valve on the context schema for the Bottling System (Appendix B) represents the set of individual valves with which the system deals.

14

- Fourth, the store symbol represents stored data shared between the system and a terminator (for example, data about the configuration of the plant, or data to be used in computations). Modification of the stored data by a terminator does not affect the system; likewise, if the system modifies the stored data, the terminators are not affected. The system must be active with respect to the store to obtain input.

- Finally, except for flows from a store, the direction of a flow indicates the direction of causality. Output flows are produced by the system, and it is the terminator's responsibility to handle the flows when they arrive. Similarly, input flows to the system are caused by terminators, and it is the system's responsibility to decide what to do when they arrive.

Although a flow from a terminator may be prompted by the system, the production of the desired flow is still the responsibility of the terminator. When, and if, the flow finally arrives from the terminator, the system must then respond to it. Note that the idea of causality refers to the responsibility for producing the flow, not to the implementation mechanism for acquiring it. An input flow means the system must accept the flow when it is "there," even if a read is required to obtain it.

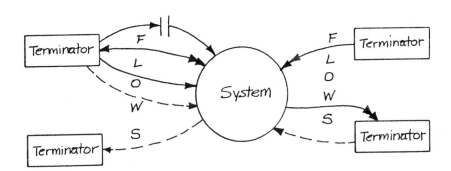

Figure 2.1 Context schema notation.

2.3 Context definition in a systems engineering environment

When a complex system is developed, all the subsystems often evolve together. In the case of a surveillance system, for example, it may be necessary to proceed with development of the embedded computer system that does the data analysis before a final decision has been made about the nature of the sensors that will capture the data. This parallel development situation presents a problem in context definition. The precise nature of the interface to the embedded system may simply not be known at development time.

The extent of this problem may be illustrated by detailing some of the complications that may occur in developing even a simple system. Consider the Cruise Control System (Appendix A). In order to function successfully, the system must perceive the motion of the automobile relative to the Earth. There are a number of ways it could do this. An inertial guidance system is costly and quite exotic by automotive standards, but it would clearly do the job. The guidance system produces a signal proportional to the acceleration of the car. The speed is the time integral of the acceleration, and thus a zero output indicates a constant speed. More realistically, the system might perceive the rotation rate of the wheels by observing the rotation of some mechanical component linked to the wheels. A feasible mechanism for doing this is to attach a magnet to the drive shaft, and to surround the shaft with another magnet. The relative motion of the magnets as the shaft rotates will produce an alternating electric current whose frequency is proportional to the rotation rate. Another feasible mechanism is a mirror affixed to the speedometer cable. If a source of light is aimed at the cable, the mirror will produce a reflected beam once per rotation that can be aimed at a photodetector. The photodetector in turn produces an electrical pulse each time it is illuminated. Although both the magnet and the mirror detection mechanisms produce an alternating electric current, the frequency corresponding to a given speed might be quite different in the two cases.

Let's now follow the sensor output as it finds its way to the embedded computer system that will use the data to keep the automobile at a constant speed. Assuming the Cruise Control System will utilize a digital processor, the inertial guidance system output would have to be digitized by an analog-digital converter before it could be used; the converter would most likely be connected to the processor by a parallel interface. The inputs of the other two sensors could (after suitable alteration or amplification) be fed into a serial input line of the processor. Alternatively, the signal could drive a pulse counter, which when triggered would provide its current count to the processor across a parallel or serial interface.

Pity the developer of the embedded system when faced with this type of uncertainty! The input signals:

- may represent either rotation rate or acceleration,

- may be input in parallel or serial mode, and

- may arrive in the form of individual pulses, pulse or digitized translations of analog signals.

As we will demonstrate in the following section, uncertainties of this kind need not preclude a rigorous definition of system boundaries, provided that the concept of implementation-dependence is properly exploited. There are two major guidelines that will assist in creating a context diagram that usefully describes the essence of a system. First, the terminators and flows should be identified from the point of view of the subject matter of the system. Second, the transformation that represents the system should be considered to exclude the interface technology.

2.4 Identification of terminators and flows

In order to examine terminator and flow identification, let's use the Bottle-Filling System (Appendix B) as an illustration. The purpose of the embedded system modeled in Figure 2.2 is to control part of the operation by maintaining the solution that is put in the bottles at the proper pH. The subject matter of this system is chemical engineering. However, the flows and terminators have names drawn mainly from computer technology and give a reader no help in understanding the fundamental nature of the system. In Figure 2.3, the problem has been corrected by renaming the flows and terminators with chemical engineering terminology.

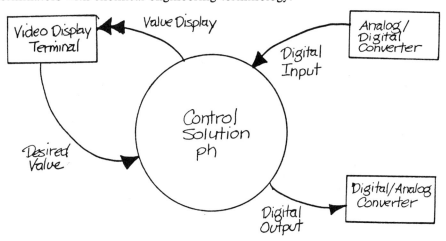

Figure 2.2 Context schema with poorly chosen names.

It is instructive to reexamine Figures 2.2 and 2.3 considering the terminology described in Chapter 1, that is, in terms of the perception/action space, sensors/actors, communication links, and processors. Figure 2.2 shows the embedded system's interaction with the communications links. Figure 2.3, on the other hand, describes interaction with things in the system's perception/action space, such as the solution, and with sensors/actors, such as the buffer inlet valve; the supervisor could be in either category. Thus, saying that the description of the system's environment has moved away from the immediate surroundings of the system and toward the perception/action space, and saying that the terminology has become more subject-matter-oriented, reflects two views of the same phenomenon. Showing the system input as Current pH rather than as Digital Input permits rigorous definition of input characteristics (for example, range and required precision of measurement), while deferring issues such as serial versus parallel to the implementation model.

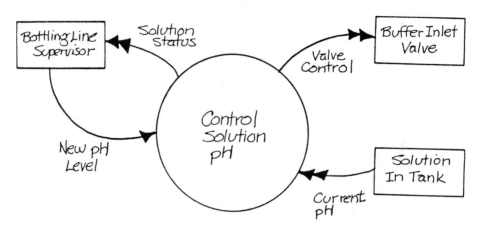

Figure 2.3 Context schema with well-chosen names.

Let's return to the observation that in Figure 2.3 the decision has been made to retain (in the case of the buffer inlet valve) some details of the actor technology. It would have been possible as an alternative to show an output called Required pH Change from the system to the Solution terminator. However, the system context seems easier to visualize from Figure 2.3 as shown. Here are some rough guidelines for making such choices. Show the sensor/actor technology when:

- the sensor/actor technology has been defined in detail;

- the sensor/actor technology is more closely related to the subject matter of the system than to the technology of computer peripheral devices;

- a sensor must be controlled by the embedded system in order to per- form its function (for example, a movable optical detector); and/or

- the nature of the data received from or sent to the environment is funda- mentally dependent on the choice of sensor or actor.

Show the objects in the system's perception/action space when:

- the sensor/actor technology is not well-defined;

- the sensor/actor technology is not closely related to the subject matter of the system (for example, general purpose I/O peripherals);

- a sensor passively sends through data about the perception space to the em- bedded system;

- the nature of the data sent to or received from the environment is relatively independent of sensor/actor technology; and/or

- the interface between the system and a human operator is being described.

The basic principle is to show the sensor/actor technology only when it is likely to be visible to the software or hardware carrying out the application-specific work of the system.

Let's now look at the second guideline for creating the context schema.

2.5 Exclusion of interface technology

It may seem superfluous to say that the transformation represented on the context schema contains no interface implementation details, since no details of the transformation are shown in any case. However, we want to show that the modeler's picture of how the interface technology relates to the context schema can affect the way the diagram is built. Consider again the relationship between Figures 2.2 and 2.3. It is tempting to think that in moving to Figure 2.3 we have *incorporated* the display terminal and the converters into our view of the system. A better way to visualize the situation — suggested by Figure 2.4 — is that interface technology *surrounds* the context diagram, separating the *real* actors, sensors, and perception/action space objects from the *virtual* actors, sensors, and objects perceived by the system. (This idea is closely related to the idea of a *virtual device* as advocated by Britton, Parker, and Parnas [1]). A specific instance of this placement of implementation technology is shown in Figure 2.5, which shows details of the current pH input from the solution terminator in Figure 2.3. This shows the sequence of transformations necessary to connect a portion of the real environment of the pH control system to its virtual environment. The box surrounding the implementation technology may be thought of as the "virtual pH sensor."

As another illustration, this time from the point of view of a human interface, we may return to Figure 2.3 and focus on the input labeled New pH Level. Now consider the actual procedure that a supervisor sitting at a video display terminal might carry out to enter a new setpoint:

(1) Hit a control key that causes display of a setpoint screen. This screen shows the current setpoint and permits overwriting it.

(2) Overwrite all or part of the current setpoint to specify a new value.

(3) Receive an error message describing any errors made such as an out-of-range value entered.

(4) Correct any errors and hit a control key indicating that the data is complete.

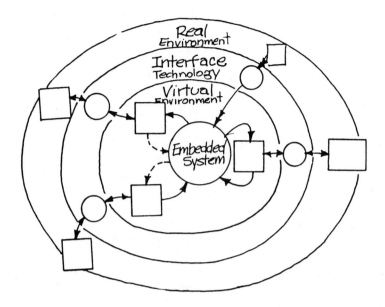

Figure 2.4 Visualization of implementation technology.

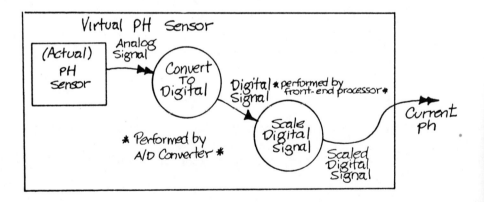

Figure 2.5 Implementation technology detail.

Notice that the user's view of the data entry procedure is quite different from the system's view (Figure 2.6) — the system's view is implementation-independent; the user's view is dependent on the implementation technology of user-system interface. For this reason, modeling the user view of the system interface is deferred to the implementation model.

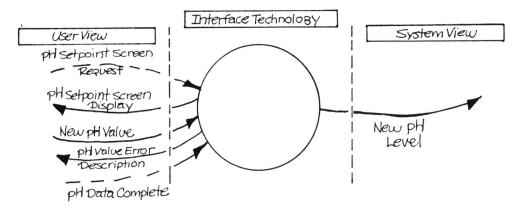

Figure 2.6 User and system views of data entry.

As with the identification conventions described in the last section, excluding interface details allows a precise description of system boundaries. The effect of this exclusion is a prescription of the required interface between the *essential* system and the world outside. The implementer is then free to choose sensors, actors, and communication links at will as long as the essential interface characteristics are preserved.

2.6 Expanded contexts — material and energy transformations

In all the examples given so far in this chapter, the terminators have been communication links, sensors/actors, or objects in the perception/action space of the system. Correspondingly, the flows have represented data or control messages between the embedded system and the terminators. We have shown that in such cases, the concept of a virtual environment for the embedded system allows development to proceed in the absence of final decisions about sensor/actor technology.

Let's now consider a different strategy. Suppose that the overall system includes transformations of material or of energy from one form to another. Suppose also that either the nature of the sensors and actors that will perform these transformations, or the details of the interface between the sensors/actors and the embedded system, are unknown. Figure 2.7 illustrates a context schema for the Bottle-Filling System (Appendix B) that would be appropriate in such a situation. The characteristics of this context schema are:

- The material/energy flows depict the objects that enter and leave the perception/action space of the system.

- The terminators that send and receive the material and energy flows are outside the perception/action space.

- The material and energy transformations are visualized as being *inside* the transformation that represents the system boundary.

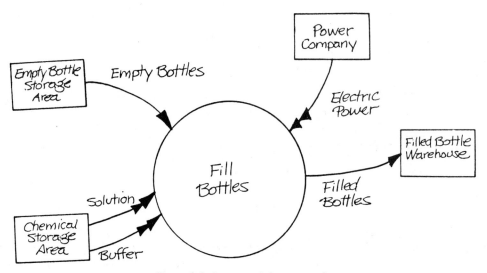

Figure 2.7 An expanded context schema.

Modeling a system in this way is often helpful in understanding data transformation requirements in a system such as a manufacturing plant, where the structure of the data and control transformations is determined by the nature of the production process. It is vital to understand the flow of material/energy in such a system, where the complexity of the manufacturing process is a barrier to an integrated view of the plant. The specification for systems of this kind is ultimately dependent on the physics, chemistry, or biology of the underlying processes.

However, the context of the embedded system must ultimately be defined for detailed development to occur. In order to carry out this "context reduction," the individual material and energy transformations must first be modeled, as illustrated by Figure 2.8. Each material or energy transformation contained within the expanded context must be reconstructed to show the objects or sensors and actors in the real world, and the embedded system with which they interact. This reconstruction is necessarily based on the technology used to carry out the material/energy transformation. The terminators shown on the resulting context schema incorporate the material transformation. This can be visualized as shown in Figure 2.9. Notice that the physical material (the solution) is now completely excluded from the embedded system, having been removed to the terminator.

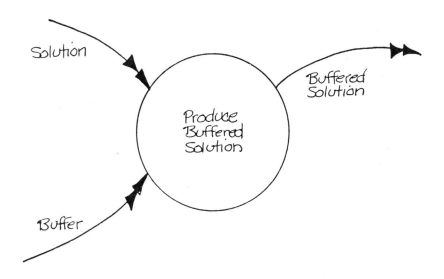

Figure 2.8 Portion of model built from expanded context schema.

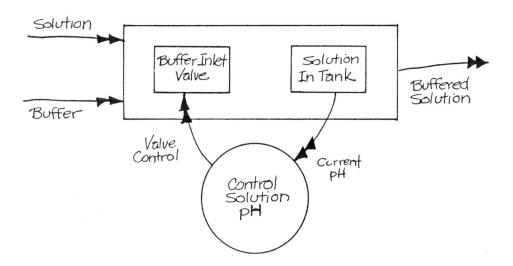

Figure 2.9 Reduction of context to exclude material transformations.

2.7 Defining context specifics

The context schema provides a definition of the boundary between a system and its environment, but it provides few details. As with the other schemas we have discussed, the specifics for the components declared on the schema must be defined. The context schema is also the highest level in the leveled model, and therefore the details of the context schema are redundant with the details of the behavioral model. However, it is helpful to begin some definition at the time we construct the context schema.

Flows and stores on the context schema play the same role as they do on the transformation schema. They have meaning, composition, and type as described in Volume 1,Chapter 11, (Specifying Data). At context definition time, however, typically only the meaning is well-understood. Composition or type definitions are often not available, in which case they must be delayed until the detailed construction of the behavioral model. The meanings of flows and stores on the context schema should be specified as a part of context definition (and, if known, so should the composition or type). Failure to define the meanings of flows and stores will make review and verification of the context schema impossible.

The terminators that appear on the context schema represent objects or sensors/actors in the system's environment with which the system interacts. Since these entities are in the system's perception/action space, the system will often need to store data about them and about their interactions. Interactions between terminators may be either active or passive. An active interaction is represented by an external event that occurs in a terminator (or terminators) and causes the system to make a response that affects the activities of other terminators. For example, Figure 2.10 shows a portion of a train control system context schema. As the trains move on the tracks, the locations of the trains are updated. Depending on the locations of other trains, the trains may be commanded to speed up or slow down as appropriate. There is thus an active interaction between the Track terminator and the Train terminator. A passive interaction exists between the Switch and the Track terminators. The location of the switches with respect to the tracks must be stored by the system so that trains may be effectively switched from track to track.

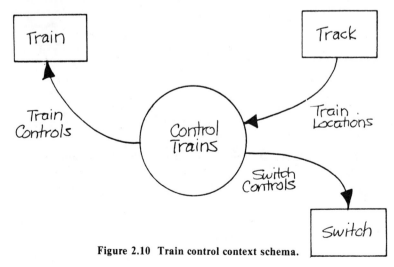

Figure 2.10 Train control context schema.

The data schema, with its associated specifics, is an appropriate tool for modeling terminators and their active and passive interactions. A preliminary data schema such as the one illustrated in Figure 2.11 may be a useful adjunct to the context schema.

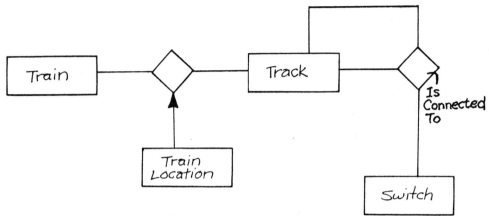

Figure 2.11 Train control preliminary data schema.

The precise behavior of the transformation on the context schema is to be described by the behavioral model. However, to aid in the construction of the behavioral model, we need to know the *purpose* or objective of the system. A short narrative text description of this purpose should be added to the context schema. The document should focus only a high-level description of the intent of the system; it should not be a description of the functional requirements — that is properly left to the behavioral model.

Finally, a description of the desired *attributes* of the system should also be added to the model. An attribute of a system is a characteristic of the system *as a whole.* For example, availability or reliability attributes, mean-time-between-failure, mean-time-to-repair, and the like describe the overall characteristics of the system in operation. Growth needs of the system, its lifetime, and maintainability characteristics also properly qualify as attributes of the system. Again, this description should not encroach on the responsibilities of the behavioral model.

Context schemas can easily become quite large, even unmanageable. To solve this problem with the transformation schema, we leveled the model to reduce complexity as described in Chapter 12 of Volume 1 (Organizing the Model). In the next two sections, we shall discuss some issues in the construction of large context schemas.

2.8 Packaging context flows

Packaging of flows is a strategy for reducing the complexity of a context schema. The fundamental guideline for packaging, as with the transformation schema, is that the internal organization of a flow should match the meaning of the flow to the system.

As an example, consider Figure 2.12, which shows several packaged flows. Tank Levels is not a helpful packaging; the system is likely to respond differently to an empty supply tank than to an empty reaction tank. (A corresponding packaging of the terminators would also suppress useful information since the tanks play different roles for the system.) On the other hand, Reaction Tank Status could also be a packaged flow (containing level and fill rate, for example), but it represents a single cohesive unit for the receiver.

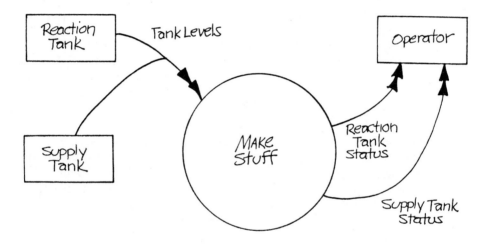

Figure 2.12 Context schema with poorly packaged flows.

Flows should be packaged when the packaged flow forms a cohesive unit of interest to the receiver.

Flows should not be packaged when:

- the flows occur asynchronously;
- the flows require a "tag" (identifier) to separate out the components on receipt; or
- the flows come from separate terminators.

2.9 Leveled and multiple-context schemas

Even if flows are packaged, the context schema is often still too large for a single screen. The solution is simple: split the diagram onto several screens. An example is shown in Figure 2.13. The several screens together make up a complete context schema. We describe the set as a leveled context schema.

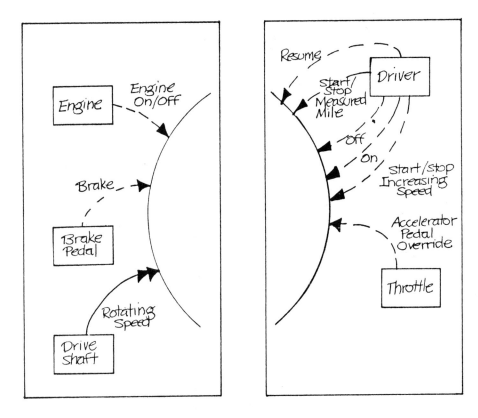

Figure 2.13 A simple leveled context schema.

An alternative approach, which is particularly useful when a development project is split into several independent teams, is to draw multiple context schemas, as illustrated in Figure 2.14. In this approach, the schemas show their connections by drawing the companion system as a terminator. Each subsystem can then be developed independently.

2.10 Summary

Context definition is a first step in defining the scope of the system; without such a definition development is difficult, if not impossible. We have introduced a notation for defining system scope and provided some heuristics for constructing the definition. Most importantly, heuristics have been provided for context construction in ill-defined environments.

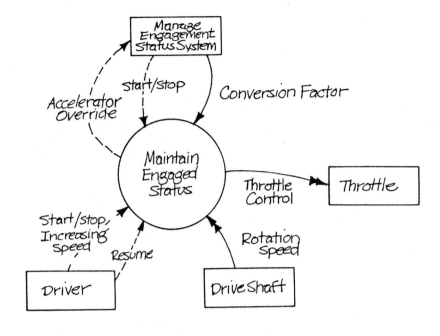

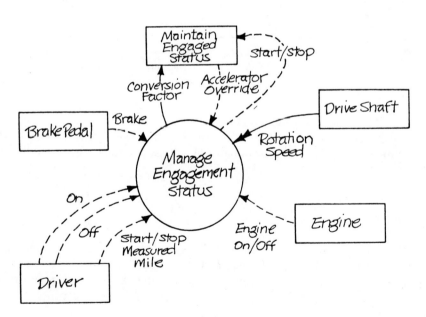

Figure 2.14 Multiple context schemas.

Chapter 2: References

1. K.H. Britton, R.A. Parker, and D.L. Parnas. *A Procedure for Designing Abstract Interfaces for Device Interface Models.* Proceedings, Fifth International Conference on Software Engineering, IEEE, 1981, pp. 195-204.

3
Modeling External Events

3.1 Introduction

As mentioned in Chapter 1 (Essential Modeling Heuristics), the central feature of the environmental model is a specification of the events to which the system must respond. In the following sections we will further explain the concept of an external event and describe methods for formulating an external event list for a system.

3.2 Definition of an external event

An event in a general sense is a significant occurrence. An *external event* has three characteristics:

- It occurs in the system's environment.

- It elicits a preplanned response from the system.

- It occurs at a specific point in time.

Let's consider each of these characteristics in turn.

For the purposes of defining external events, the system's environment is represented by the terminators on the context schema. Any occurrence that arises within the transformation representing the system is internal and does not qualify as an external event. Figure 3.1 shows a context schema for the SILLY logic analyzer (Appendix C). Assume that the logic analyzer is in the process of collecting data from the microprocessor. Consider the two candidate events User Requests Termination of Logic Acquisition and Logic States are Displayed. The first of the two originates with the user and thus occurs outside the system boundary; it therefore qualifies as an external event. The second, even though it is a response to the first, originates within the system and thus fails to satisfy the above definition.

To investigate the idea of a preplanned response, imagine that in the situation illustrated in Figure 3.1, while SILLY is collecting data, the microprocessor's clock suddenly changes frequency and begins emitting pulses at double the previous rate. Sophisticated logic analyzers, in fact, are capable of measuring and recording the intervals between timing pulses in the devices they monitor. SILLY, however, is a simple system and merely responds to the occurrence of the microprocessor clock pulse by capturing the data on the leads. Therefore, it has no preplanned response to a change in the external clock frequency. If the system can "keep up" with the new clock rate, it will not respond in any way to the change, but will simply continue

30

collecting data at each clock pulse. If the faster frequency exceeds the system's ability to finish collecting one set of data before the next arrives, SILLY *will* respond, but in an unpredictable, unplanned way — by sporadically missing data collections. Although the speed-up occurs in the system's environment, it fails to satisfy the definition of an external event on the preplanned response criterion.

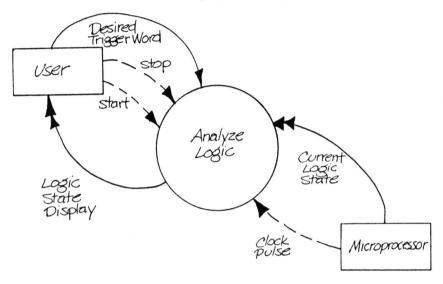

Figure 3.1 SILLY context schema.

To understand the third criterion — that an external event occurs at a specific point in time — it is necessary to recall the distinction between time-discrete data flows and time-continuous data flows discussed in Volume 1, Chapter 6. Consider the context schema of Figure 3.2, which describes a typical transaction-oriented system. It is easy to picture the external events in this system as coinciding with the arrival of discrete data flows. The events — Customer Makes Deposit and Customer Makes Withdrawal Request — can (at least with regard to the completion of the input) be localized to a point in time.

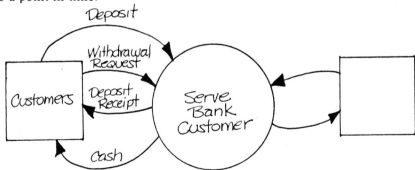

Figure 3.2 Transaction-oriented system.

As an alternative, consider the aircraft on-board system illustrated in Figure 3.3. It is tempting to say that Aircraft is Climbing is an event. The climbing certainly occurs in the system's environment, and the system presumably responds at least by periodically recording the rate of climb. However, the event cannot be localized as occurring at a specific point in time. To be useful for event modeling purposes, an event that involves a continuous data flow must describe a transition from one discrete mode of behavior to another. An event that is relevant in this context and that satisfies the external event definition is Aircraft Stops Climbing, presuming that the system responds in some specific way when the rate of climb reaches zero. It might be argued that, after all, the rate of climb is simply a continuous variable and that a zero rate of climb is simply one value among many others both positive and negative. However, this argument will be singularly unconvincing to a pilot, to whom there is a very significant real-world difference between a positive and a negative rate of climb and thus a great importance attached to the transition. This is another illustration of the basic idea that an essential model describes a system in subject-matter terms.

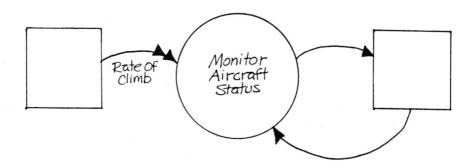

Figure 3.3 Aircraft on-board system.

This distinction between time-continuous and time-discrete behaviors is critical to modeling events in real-time systems. Consider the two transformations of Figure 3.4, which describe a part of the Bottle-Filling System (Appendix B). It is possible to think of each possible change in pH value for the Change pH to New Value subsystem as a distinct event. However, if there are N distinct values, even restricting changes to adjacent values results in 2(N-1) possible events. To the person concerned with process control these events are all merged into a continuous behavior called "ramping," just as all the possible input and output value changes of the Maintain pH at Constant Value subsystem are part of a continuous behavior called "maintaining a setpoint." In identifying the external events related to the behaviors, it is necessary to ask, What causes these transformations to start operating and stop operating? In the case of Figure 3.4, the event Operator Enters New pH Value might start Change pH to New Value, and the event pH Reaches New Value would stop Change pH to New Value and start Maintain pH at Constant Value.

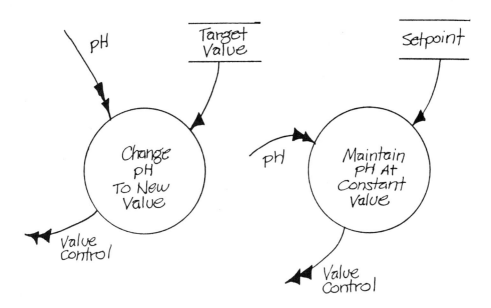

Figure 3.4 Two continuous transformations.

Now that we've discussed the definition of an external event, let's look at the difference between the occurrence of an event and the system's discovery that an event has occurred.

3.3 Events versus event recognition

Let's return to our discussion of Figure 3.4 and ask why pH reaches New Value is an external event. After all, the system can't determine that it needs to make a response before comparing the pH data with a stored internal value (Figure 3.5). We'll defend our identification first by appealing to the definition. The reaching of the desired new value certainly happens in the system's environment (the liquid whose pH is being measured isn't within the embedded system for obvious reasons!), the system must make a response when the event occurs, and reaching the new pH value can be localized to a point in time. Despite the formal applicability of the definition, however, there's an important distinction to be made. In the SILLY system in Figure 3.1, the acceptance of the Stop event flow is equivalent to the system's recognition that an event has occurred. Similarly, in Figure 3.2 the arrival of the Deposit and Withdrawal Request flows are all the system needs to determine that the corresponding events have occurred. In both these cases, the event recognition is *direct*. In the case of pH Reaches New Value, there is an *indirect* recognition mechanism involving comparison of a continuous input with a value retained in a data store.

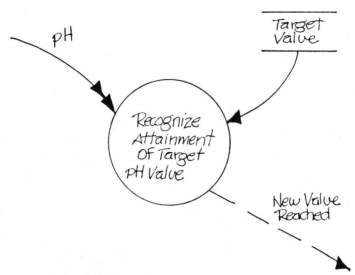

Figure 3.5 Event recognition by value comparison.

Comparison with a stored data value is only one of many possible indirect recognition mechanisms.   Consider the Defect Inspection System pictured in Appendix D. In order to fulfill its purpose, an embedded system controlling this apparatus must differentiate scanner data belonging to each individual sheet, trigger the cutter at the appropriate time, and operate the router to separate good and bad sheets. One can say that the system must respond to the events Sheet Reaches Scanner, Sheet Reaches Cutter, and Sheet Reaches Router. However, the only information relating to the sheets that the system receives concerns the motion of the conveyer mechanism. Given an external synchronization signal, which identifies that the first sheet of a roll is at the scanner, the system can then proceed to *simulate* the arrival of sheets at various points by measuring the motion of the conveyor and thus the metal. The situation is illustrated in Figure 3.6. The relative positions of the scanner, cutter, and routing mechanism must of course be part of the transformations for the simulation to work successfully. If, instead of monitoring conveyer motion, the system were to receive sensor pulses as sheets reached specific points (say by notching the roll at sheet edges and using a contact probe), neither the basic event nor the required response would change — only the recognition mechanism would differ.

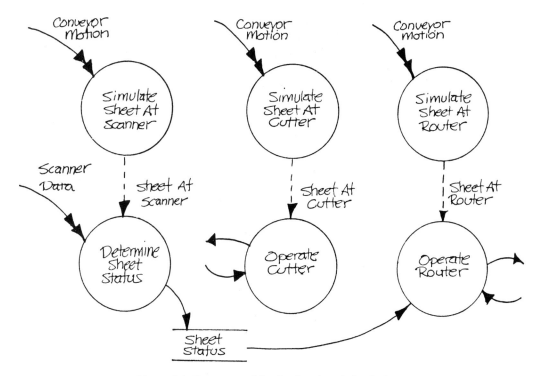

Figure 3.6 Event recognition by time-based simulation.

Another form of external event recognition is through the use of time. Imagine a production control system that produces a management report containing data about each production run and the defects on the products produced. The data required for the report should be entirely available from stored data, and the production of the report could be prompted by the manager requiring it. Alternatively, and more likely, the report might be produced at fixed intervals. In this case, there is no external flow that causes the report to be produced; nevertheless, Management Requires Production Run Report should still be regarded as an external event. Returning to our definition, the event occurs at a specific point in time and it elicits a preplanned response from the system. The remaining question is: Does the event occur in the system's environment? We argue that the requirement to produce the report is externally imposed on the system. To distinguish this type of event from other events, we call this a *temporal event*. To illustrate this, let us consider an alternative: each time a defect occurs, the report is produced in response. Unless the plant is running very smoothly this will produce outputs often enough to cause consternation and rapid modification of the system to produce less-frequent outputs: definitely something that occurs in the system's environment! Please note that there is no necessary distinction in the response between the temporal event described and the event signaled by a prompt type of flow. However, if the manager could request the report by providing a flow that contained a start date for the report's data the response would be different from that for the periodic report, and so would require another event.

3.4 Identification of individual events

In order to create a useful event list, some guidelines are necessary. Imagine, for example, a complex data communications system with a variety of input event flows. To say that there is a single event called Input Signal Arrives is to miss the point entirely. The fundamental guideline, in fact, is that events must be described in subject-matter terminology — a variation on a familiar theme. In the data communications case the events might be Transmission is Requested, Receipt is Acknowledged, and so on.

A useful way to determine whether a candidate event associated with a discrete data flow or event flow is better described as a collection of events is to see whether the flow contains an explicit or implicit "tag" as discussed in Section 2.8 in Chapter 2 (Defining System Context). In the SILLY system the candidate event, User Provides Control Input, cannot be responded to until the system decides whether the input was a Start or a Stop. Therefore there are two events, User Requests Start and User Requests Stop.

In the case of an event associated with a discrete *data* flow, a useful question is, Do all instances of the event involve the same set of data elements? If a piece of data is present in some instances and absent in others, the response may differ in the two cases and there may be two events involved. This idea also extends to different *ranges* of a data element that have different significances. The filing of a flight plan that involves crossing a secured military area might evoke a different response from a system than the filing of one that involves only non-sensitive terrain.

Let's now explore some general strategies for creating a list of events.

3.5 The active event modeling approach

The existence of a reasonably well-defined context schema suggests an active modeling approach to the problem — in other words, that we *visualize the system in action* to identify events. In this procedure, the terminators are thought of as transformations that actively send flows to and receive flows from the system. The events are then derived by determining what effects the actions of the terminators can have on the system. Of course some events are identified with the arrival of discrete inputs and can be identified in a straightforward way. Questions that might be asked include: What would cause the system to begin producing that continuous output from this continuous input? What would cause the system to start (or stop) accepting occurrences of this discrete input? What would cause the system to produce an instance of this discrete output? Are there significant values of this input that will cause an event if reached? Do certain occurrences of this input cause different responses from other occurrences?

Returning to the context schema for the SILLY system in Figure 3.1, applying the active modeling approach yields in part:

(1) User starts acquisition

(2) Non-trigger state occurs at clock pulse

(3) Trigger State occurs at clock pulse

(4) 128th state following trigger state occurs at clock pulse

The third event involves a significant value of the Logic State input, and the fourth event causes the system to stop accepting Clock inputs and to display the Logic States. Notice that Clock Pulse Occurs is not a single event, since the system's response varies according to an indirect recognition mechanism involving checking the trigger word and counting clock pulses.

3.6 The passive event modeling approach

The method described in the previous section required the system to have well-defined terminators and input/output connections. Suppose that an event list must be built in the absence of a precise context. This is not an unrealistic premise. In fact, a practical way of attacking the problem might require the terminators and flows to be derived from the events. In this case, a passive modeling approach, which involves a *search for associations between objects in the system's environment*, can be used.

The starting point is a list that includes at least the sensors and actors used by the embedded system and the objects in the perception/action space that are perceived and acted upon. In the instance of a system that is part of a larger system, the things perceived and acted upon might also be (or contain) sensors and actors, and the list can be expanded by including a broader perception/action space. Consider a communications system for military reconnaissance. The sensors and actors include radio transmitters and receivers, and reconnaissance aircraft and ships are perceived and acted upon. However, the reconnaissance planes and ships themselves contain sensors and actors, such as infrared and optical sensors, which in turn perceive reconnaissance targets such as troop concentrations. Things perceived by a sensor are not restricted to physical objects. A human acting as a sensor can perceive abstract things such as desired situations, requirements, standards, and so on which are legitimate list entries. The list just described is used to build a data schema in which the entries on the list become the object types and the associations among list entries are the relationships. All of the ideas and guidelines provided in Volume 1, Chapter 10 (Modeling Stored Data), can be used in building the schema. A candidate event for passive event modeling is an activity or operation that causes a relationship to be formed or deleted on the data schema.

As an example, let's look at the Bottle-Filling system. The list items for the sensor/actor technology include Bottle-Filling Valve, Bottle Release Mechanism, and pH Sensor. The perception/action space includes Bottle, Solution, and Bottling-Line Operator. The operator, as a sensor, has a perception/action space that involves Production Requirements and Product Standards. To build the data schema we take these entries pairwise or in small groups and identify the associations among them (Figure 3.7). An association of interest between the bottle and the bottle-filling valve is alignment. The operations that create and delete this association are, respectively, Bottle Comes into Alignment with Valve and Bottle Moves out of Alignment with Valve, which are then potential events to which the system might respond. The Selected relationship between Operator and Product Standard means that the operator has identified one of the instances of Product Standard (that is, a target pH of the solution) as governing the production process. The operation of changing from one standard to another removes the connection to one instance of the standard and adds a new one. Thus Operator Selects New Product Standard is a potential event.

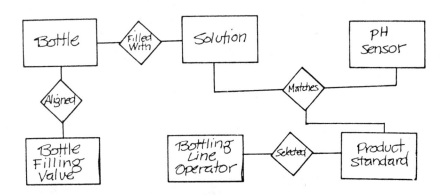

Figure 3.7 Data schema for bottling system.

3.7 The brainstorming approach to event modeling

It should be clear from the preceding two sections that the strategies for building event lists are not precise analytical approaches but simply rough-and-ready aids to the thought process. The identification of a complete set of events is a critical point in the requirements definition process. The failure to identify an important event will not appear as a deficiency in the formal notation for modeling the system — a system model can be perfectly reasonable and technically consistent yet still fail to identify a desirable event response. The end result, however, will be a system that operates correctly (that is, matches the model) but whose behavior does not meet end-user expectations.

The only defense against this potential problem is to take a "brainstorming" approach to building an event list. The list should be created by a group, and the group should not consider its work done until every conceivable event to which the system might respond, no matter how far-fetched, has been examined and accepted or rejected [1].

One class of events frequently missed relates to "failure mode" operations of a system. Although the essential model should not deal with imperfections in the technology used to implement the *system transformation*, it *must* deal with potential problems with the technology of the devices and systems shown as terminators. Since the terminators are by definition outside the bounds of the system-building effort represented by the model, the implementers cannot modify the terminator technology at will to improve its reliability. Instead, they must build responses to terminator problems into the essential model of the system. A useful approach to modeling responses to terminator problems is to build a list of "normal" events and then to ask, for each event, Does the system need to respond if this event fails to occur as expected?

As an illustration, let's return once again to the SILLY system of Figure 3.1. The partial event list given earlier in the chapter lists several events involving a microprocessor clock pulse. But what if an expected clock pulse fails to occur? Should the system have a time-out mechanism that produces a message to the user if a pulse isn't received within some time interval? Another event mentions the identification of a trigger state. What if the system runs for an extended period of time without a trigger state being found? Such questions are very useful for probing the adequacy of an event list.

3.8 Summary

The identification of the events to which a system must respond is critical to requirements definition. An external event has been defined as something arising in the system's environment at a specific point in time and requiring a preplanned response. In the next chapter, the identified events will be used to create a detailed model of system behavior.

Chapter 3: References

1. J. Clark, S. Mellor, and P. Ward, "An Application of Event Modeling to the Specification of an Avionics Simulator." Paper Presented at Structured Development Forum VI, Long Beach, February 1985.

4
Deriving the Behavioral Model

4.1 Introduction

The context schema and its associated specifics, together with the external event list and the environmental data schema, if one is built, constitute a detailed model of a system's environment. Clearly this model does not contain all the details necessary to build a detailed description of the system's behavior. Nevertheless, the environmental model provides a basis for constructing the behavioral model, and in this chapter we lay out the guidelines for doing so.

4.2 An informal high-level requirements model

Our task in building the behavioral model is very simple: *We must describe the response made by the system to each event in the external event list.* A very direct way of approaching this assignment is to describe the responses informally in narrative text. The results can be organized in the form of a two-column list that shows each event in the left-hand column and the corresponding response in the right-hand column. The description of the response must include at least:

- the most common or most likely response to the event;

- alternate responses and the conditions under which they are made; and

- conditions under which the system will not respond to the event.

A package that includes a context schema, a statement of purpose, and a list of events with narrative response descriptions is a very useful informal specification of requirements. It could be considered as a preliminary deliverable for purposes of project management. In addition, it might be the *only* system description necessary for high-level review and "sign-off" by managers who need only understand the system in general terms. An example of a package of this type for the SILLY system would include Table 4.1 along with Figure 4.1.

Clearly the package just described is not a rigorous specification of the behavior of the proposed system. There is no information, for instance, on the use of the system inputs shown on the context schema by the various event responses. In addition, there are no rigorous criteria for deciding whether a response is satisfactory, such as required quantitative relationships between output values and corresponding input values. To fill in these details, a notation more formal than narrative text must be used to specify the responses. We shall, of course, use the transformation schema and data schema.

41

Event	Response
User Starts Acquisition	Start Recording Logic States and Look for Trigger Word
User Stops Acquisition	Stop Recording Logic States and Display States Recorded so far.
User Enters Trigger Word	Store Trigger Word; Ignore If Logic Acquisition In Progress.
Trigger Word Found.	Store Next 128 Logic States; Then stop and Display States Recorded.

Table 4.1 Informal requirements model events and responses.

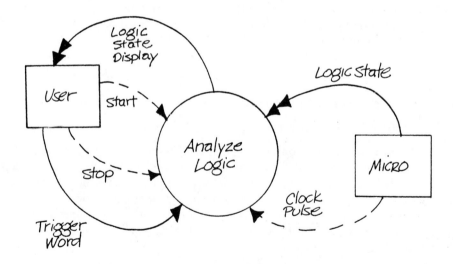

Figure 4.1 Informal requirements model — context schema.

4.3 Systems dominated by a specific perspective

We showed in Chapters 6 and 10 of Volume 1 that there are two fundamentally different perspectives one can take in describing a system. The active view, which we expressed by the transformation schema, pictures the system as a mechanism for transforming inputs into outputs. The passive view, for which we used the data schema, sees a system in terms of the associations among real-world things that it must keep track of. All systems that are built from computer hardware and software components transform inputs into outputs, and virtually all systems need to create or remember data about their environments. However, the relative importance of these two aspects varies widely from system to system.

Imagine a system that collects data about the flight plans filed by all the aircraft over a large region, and uses this data to derive statistics about arrival and departure patterns at particular airports by time of day or by type of aircraft, traffic densities in various regions of the airspace, and so on. The transformation schema of Figure 4.2 illustrates such a system in general terms. Notice that the transformation structure of this system follows a pattern that is typical of all data storage and retrieval systems; it consists of one group of transformations that puts data into storage, and another group that extracts stored data and creates outputs. The focus of the storage transformations will be on the patterns and validation rules of data as it arrives from the reporting sources, and the focus of the retrieval transformations will be on identifying specific data associations and transforming them into outputs.

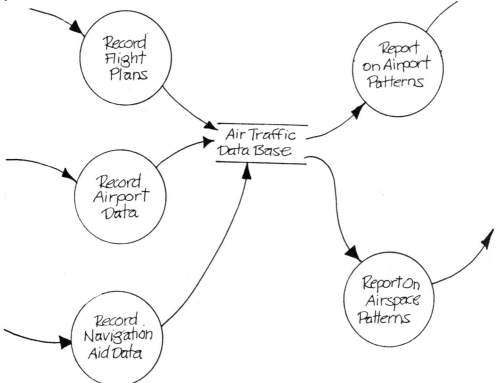

Figure 4.2 Air traffic analysis system transformation schema.

This perspective is not as broad nor as illuminating as the *structure of real-world associations* between aircraft, airports, runways, navigation markers, and so on that constitutes the basic subject matter of the system and that is illustrated in Figure 4.3. Therefore, a data schema should be of more assistance to the developer for this type of system than a transformation schema. It is fair to call systems of this type *stored-data-driven.*

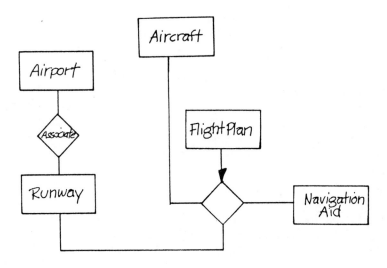

Figure 4.3 Data schema for Figure 4.2.

Pure data storage and retrieval systems, of course, don't typically fall into the real-time category. However, a process control system with rather modest control requirements may have elaborate requirements for collecting, correlating, and analyzing data about the processes controlled. Such a system might also be stored-data-driven.

In contrast, consider the bottling system described in Appendix B and shown in simplified form in Figure 4.4. In a mechanical sense the world surrounding the embedded system might have quite an elaborate structure — the bottle-handling machinery and the liquid flow connections between the storage tank and the filling valves might be quite complex. However, many of these complexities are irrelevant to the system as it performs its specific functions of controlling pH, opening and closing valves, and so on. The real-world associations that the system must keep track of are less illuminating to the developer than its *operations* — the patterns by which it transforms continuous inputs into continuous outputs. This type of system is characterized as *transformation-driven.*

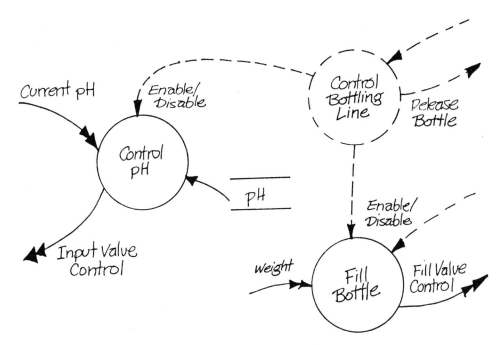

Figure 4.4 Bottling filling system (partial).

There is a large class of systems for which the data schema and the transformation schema are about equally important in terms of the insight that they provide for the modeler. But in cases where one view or the other is dominant, an early focus on the dominant view should facilitate the development process.

The event list can be used to decide whether the data schema or the transformation schema is likely to dominate. A stored-data-driven system has events that fall into one of two categories. The first category is a real-world event to which the system responds by storing data. In the air traffic analysis system of Figures 4.2 and 4.3 such events might be Pilot Files Flight Plan, Airport Changes Landing Pattern, or Navigation Marker Relocated. The second category consists of requests for analytical data in which the inputs (if any) simply identify the stored data to be extracted and manipulated. An event of this type might be Analysis of Airport Arrival Pattern is Requested.

The majority of events in a transformation-driven system will require a response that uses *current* inputs to produce *immediate* outputs and store data only incidentally. In the bottle-filling case, such events are Operator Initiates pH Control (by starting the system, for example) and Bottle Arrives at Filling Valve.

A system developer can examine the event list for events fitting these descriptions and use this information to decide whether to build the transformation schema first, to build the data schema first, or to build both schemas together. In the remaining sections of this chapter we will address first the building of the transformation schema and then the building of the data schema.

4.4 Representing behavior on the transformation schema

Required behavior can often be represented on the transformation schema in either data transformation or state transition terms. Consider the event Quantity of Inventory Item is Issued in relation to the system modeled in Figures 1.5, 1.6, and 1.7 Chapter 1. If the state transition representation (Figure 1.6) is chosen, an inventory issue that drives the quantity to zero will cause a change of state and will prevent the system from responding to future issues of that item until a receipt occurs. In fact, the event list should include Item Goes out of Stock, an event that requires an indirect recognition mechanism. On the other hand, if the data transformation representation (Figure 1.7) is chosen, no occurrence of an issue transaction will prevent the system from dealing with any other issue transaction. The output of a Negative Issue Verification is just one possible outcome of the functional behavior of Record Issue of Item.

Before we begin building the transformation schema, it is useful to choose between these alternative representations for responses to each event.

The intent of making these decisions regarding the representation is twofold. First, choosing the simplest adequate representation for the behavior of a system promotes easy production of the model and encourages detailed review. Second, having some view of the response representation to be used, however arbitrary, is helpful in completing the event list. In the example cited above, the choice of a state transition representation for the response to an issue of stock causes the modeler to add an event Item Goes Out of Stock to distinguish between the different subresponses to the issue of an item.

Our experience indicates that in most cases it is clear which representation to choose, although occasionally the two approaches produce models of about equal utility. It is often appropriate to represent responses in data transformation form when:

- the event is associated with the arrival of a discrete data flow;

- the expression of the response applies to many possible data values;

- terminators were chosen as objects in the system's perception/action space;

- there are many instances of the object in the environment.

Conversely, a response is better represented in state transition form if:

- the event is associated with continuous data flows that require an indirect event recognition mechanism, or the event is associated with event flows;

- the expression of the response is significantly different for different data values;

- terminators consist of sensor/actor technology in the system's environment;

- there are few or single instances of the object in the environment (whether represented directly, or indirectly via sensor/actor technology).

In many cases, portions of a response satisfy criteria from both groups. For example, an event flow may signal an event whose response can be expressed as a transformation on a set of continuous data values. In this case the event flow would be managed by a control transformation and its associated state transition diagram whose output event flows would enable and disable a data transformation that embodies the functional response.

4.5 Regions of the transformation schema

Before dealing with detailed guidelines for translating a context schema and an event list into a transformation schema, we'll attempt to describe the transformation schema in terms of its overall relationship to the event view of the world. Figure 4.5 shows the transformation schema as being divided into two major regions. (This figure, by the way, can be considered as an expanded view of the Embedded System bubble in Figure 2.4 of Chapter 2, Defining System Context). The outer region deals with *recognizing* events that the system needs to respond to. Transformations that can be labeled as *event recognizers* form a buffer between the system's environment and the portions of the schema that respond to the events. Event recognizer X in Figure 4.5, for example, identifies a situation in which continuous input flow A has crossed a stored value boundary (say, a temperature has exceeded a danger point) and produces an output event flow that signals that the event has occurred. Event recognizers may also operate by *simulating* the occurrence of an event based on a time delay. Event recognizer Y in Figure 4.5 accepts event flow D, and produces an output event flow E after a time T_e and an output event flow F after a time T_f. (The two outputs could also be shown as being produced by two separate transformations.) T_e is the *amount of time following the occurrence of D after which the system will assume that E has occurred;* a similar definition applies to T_f.

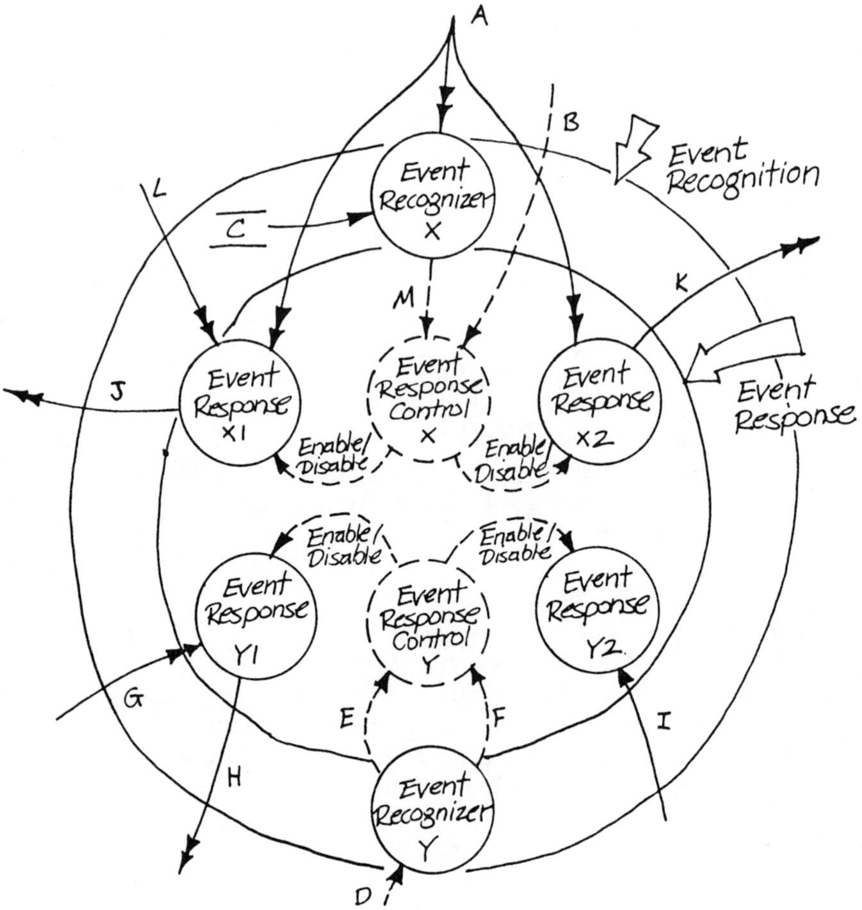

Figure 4.5 Regions of a transformation schema.

There is an important reason for separating the event recognition portion of the transformation schema from the event response portion. Although the entire essential model is implementation-independent, different portions of the model have different levels of invariance. The mechanism that recogizes the event can be changed (say by replacing the internal recognition mechanism with an external source of an event flow) without changing the definition of the event or the desired system response. The separation of the schema into two regions highlights the relatively fixed nature of the inner region, and is an application of the general heuristic of independence of parts discussed in Chapter 4 of Volume 1.

4.6 Classifying events

Before building a transformation schema, it is useful to ask a series of questions for each event on the event list.

First, how is the event perceived by the system? For example, there may be a direct correspondence between the event occurring in the environment and the arrival of a single discrete flow. The flow may be an event flow, whose name closely matches the name of the event, or it may be a discrete data flow. As we discussed in Volume 1, Chapter 6 (The Transformation Schema), a discrete data flow implicitly has two components: the data content that makes up the flow, and an associated "trigger." The name of the flow will describe the meaning of the *data* to the system, and the triggering aspect of the flow is only implied. The triggering aspect corresponds to the event in the same manner as does an event flow; that is, the arrival of the flow signals the event. We classify this type of event as *flow-direct*.

If the event cannot be perceived directly by the system, some event recognition mechanism will be required. Event recognizers produce an event flow that signals the event by examining continuous data flow(s) for particular values or combinations of values, or by comparing data flows to stored data. Please note that an event flow may require an event recognition mechanism. A typical example is a pulsed event flow such as the shaft encoder pulse in the Defect Inspection System (Appendix D). Every occurrence of the shaft encoder pulse does not correspond to an event; only those which signal that a sheet has reached a position of interest to the system constitute an event. This type of event in which a flow triggers an event recognition mechanism that in turn triggers a response is classified as *flow-indirect*.

One other type of perception mechanism may be identified. In this case, the event is indirectly recognized by the passage of time. A daily report on the progress of production in a production control system is an example. We include in this class events whose occurrence can be thought of as measured from an absolute clock (the need for the daily report), and those whose occurrence is measured relatively (say a timeout), as well as scheduled events that are recognized by examining stored data to detect the arrival of a previously-stored time (such as a production schedule). These events are classified as *temporal*.

After identifying the perception mechanism, a second question should be asked; will the occurrence of this event prevent or permit the system to respond to another occurrence of the same or another event? If an event can affect the response to other events, there must be a control component to the system's response — that is, there must be a control transformation that recognizes the occurrence of the event, and will activate and deactivate other sets of transformations in response. (It is useful at this point to identify the dependent events.) On the other hand, if the event in question does not affect other events, then there is no control component; the response is simply a data transformation. (This is common in commercial systems.)

The third question is, Will the occurrence of other events prevent or permit the system's responding to this event? A positive answer to this question implies that the response is in some way managed by a control transformation; the response may be a data transformation or the production of an event flow. (It is useful at this point to identify the events on which this event depends.) If the event is independent of the previous occurrence of all other events, the response is simply a data transformation. (Again, this is common in commercial systems.)

The fourth and final question is, Which event group does this event belong to? By asking whether a given event is dependent on other events, and whether other events are dependent on it, we can think about associated events as belonging to groups. Rarely are events divided into completely independent groups. However, it is often possible to create a good preliminary partitioning by examining the dependencies identified from the previous two questions.

The classification of events described here provides us with a starting point for building a preliminary transformation model, which we will describe in the next three sections.

4.7 The preliminary transformation model

A preliminary transformation model is intended to lay out the overall structure of a system. The model consists of a transformation schema with state-transition diagrams for any control transformations. (This model fulfills the conditions for schematic execution described in Chapter 9 of Volume 1 (Executing the Transformation Schema), and can thus be verified as qualitatively correct.)

The preliminary transformation schema should have a "flat" (unleveled) construction, with each transformation at approximately the same level of detail and with minimum interfaces between the transformations. For a medium-to-large system, this schema will contain a large number of transformations and will ultimately require leveling to attain a verifiable, reviewable form.

The state transition diagram(s) will describe the logic of the control transformation(s) embedded in the preliminary schema. Each diagram will represent the time-dependent interactions among a set of closely related events.

The next two sections describe the construction of the state transition diagrams and of the preliminary schema. No order is implied; it is possible to build the schema first, to build the state transition diagrams first, or to construct both components simultaneously.

4.8 Constructing state transition diagrams from an event list

The overall organization of a state transition diagram can be derived directly from the interactions among the external events. The dependencies among the events are determined by answering questions two and three noted in Section 4.6 of this chapter. Event list interactions can also be explained in terms of the basic logical constructs of sequence, alternation, and repetition.

Consider the Bottle-Filling System (Appendix B). The events Bottle Drops Into Place, Bottle Becomes Full, and Operator Removes Bottle form a sequence for a particular bottling line. Under normal circumstances, the events will occur in the order given and no other event on the list will intervene. The sequence of events leads directly to a sequence of states, as illustrated in Figure 4.6. The events become the conditions that lead to the changes of state.

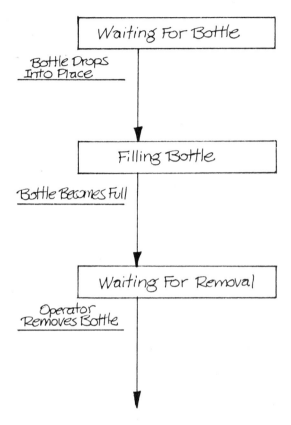

Figure 4.6 A sequence of states.

A single event, or a sequence of events, often is repeated a number of times within the operation of a system. The three events just mentioned for the Bottle-Filling System form a "loop" that is repeated for each bottle. This repetition is reflected in the state diagram as a transition back to a previous state in the sequence (Figure 4.7).

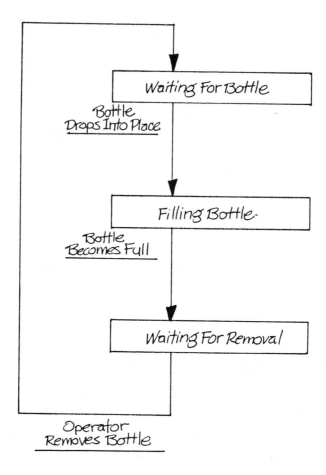

Figure 4.7 A repeating group of states.

Finally, a set of two or more events can be alternatives as successors to another event; Bottle Becomes Full can be followed by either Operator Removes Bottle or by Operator Turns Line Off. Alternatives are represented on a state diagram by multiple transitions leaving a state, as illustrated in Figure 4.8. Alternatives within an event list may also occur on a larger scale. An event and a group of events, or two groups of events, may be alternatives in the sense that they are mutually exclusive over some time period. For instance, the event Operator Sets New Bottle Size and the group Bottle Drops into Place, Bottle Becomes Full, Operator Removes Bottle are mutually exclusive. During the period of time when changing bottle size is allowed (that is, when a line is off) the three events in the group are prohibited from occurring.

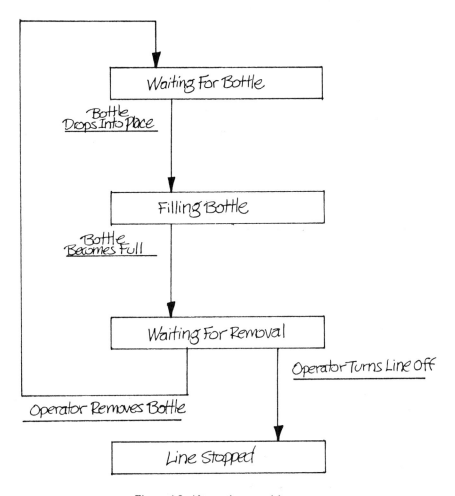

Figure 4.8 Alternative transitions.

Unless a system is unusually simple, it will be necessary to create a group of state diagrams for convenient representation. One useful partitioning strategy involves mutually exclusive groups of events as discussed in the previous paragraph. In this case, a set of states is created for each group of events, and is enabled or disabled by a "higher-level" group of states dealing with the controlling events (Figure 4.9). Another convenient strategy is to identify separate groups of sensors/actors or perception/action space objects in the system's environment, and to build a set of states for each group. For example, in the Bottle-Filling System it might be helpful to separate the states and events dealing with the pH of the product in the tank from the states and events dealing with the bottle-filling machinery.

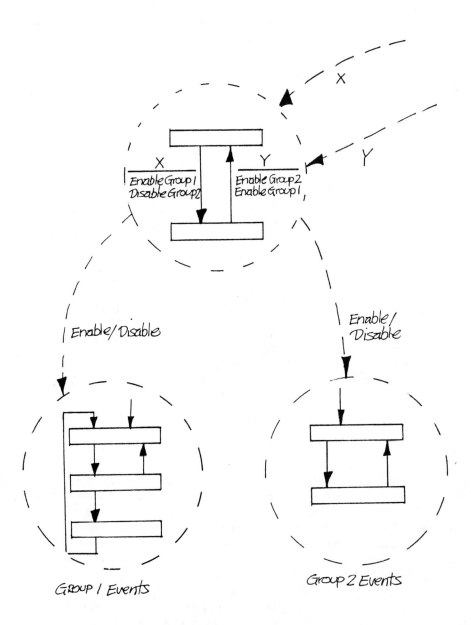

**Figure 4.9 Multiple state transition diagrams for mutually exclusive
event groups.**

If you examine the names given to the states in the preceding few figures, you will find that they represent either something in the environment that is being anticipated (for example, Waiting For Bottle) or something in the environment that is happening, possibly under system control (for example, Filling Bottle). Names such as these tie the internal behavior of the system to elements in the system's environment and we recommend using them.

If you examine the states in the last few examples, you will also notice that they represent time intervals whose starting and stopping points are determined by externally imposed requirements. The duration of the Filling Bottle state is determined only by the bottle-filling apparatus (supply lines, valves, and so on). No change in the technology of the embedded system (for example, increasing the processor speed) can change the duration of these time intervals. The translation from event list to state transition diagram thus preserves the implementation-independence of the essential model.

One common situation encountered in translating events to a state diagram violates the pattern just mentioned. Let's once again look at the Bottle-Filling System. The system's response to Operator Turns Line On is conditional; the system will only turn the line on if the bottle contact is off. Thus the event Operator Turns Line On must trigger an examination of the bottle contact status, which in turn triggers one of two subsidiary event flows (Bottle Contact Is Off or Bottle Contact Is On). The destination state of the system depends on which subsidiary event flow occurs, as shown in Figure 4.10. The state between Line Off and Line On cannot be named in terms of the system's environment. The only descriptive name would be something like Checking Bottle Contact. Furthermore, the duration of the state is inherently implementation-dependent; a faster processor will decrease the duration of the state. We will use the convention of omitting the names of such "transitory states" to emphasize their different character.

4.9 Constructing data and control transformations from an event list

The simplest connection between an event and a data transformation occurs when an event is coincident with the arrival of a discrete data flow. In this case a transformation accepts the data flow and produces whatever outputs or stored data changes are appropriate. If the system's response depends on the occurrence of other events, the data transformation must be enabled and disabled by a control transformation. This situation is illustrated for the Bottle-Filling System by Figure 4.11.

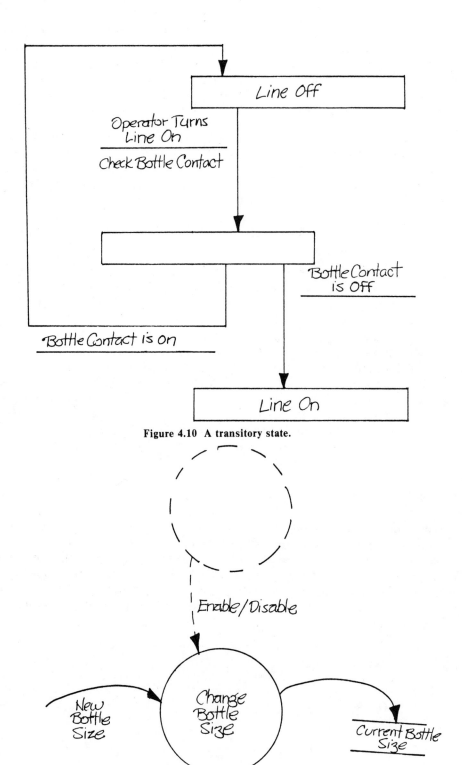

Figure 4.10 A transitory state.

Figure 4.11 A simple event response.

Another common connection between an event and a data transformation occurs when an event causes the system to begin transforming a continuous input into a continuous output. In Figure 4.12, the event flow Bottle Contact Goes On causes a control transformation to enable a data transformation accepting Weight and producing Bottle Filling Valve Control. The response may be conditional on the occurrence of other events, in which case the control transformation will produce the Enable in response to Bottle Contact Goes On only in certain states.

It is possible for an event to provoke more than one response. For example, an event flow in a process control system might enable two or more transformations of continuous inputs into continuous outputs (control loops).

Although event flows sometimes cross the boundary from the environment to the system, it is often necessary for the system to generate the event flow internally by means of an event-recognizing transformation. The Bottle Contact Goes On event flow in Figure 4.12 results from a change of value of the continuous input flow Bottle Contact. Figure 4.13 is an expansion of Figure 4.12 to show the event recognizer. Event recognition is typically a more complex process than simply identifying a value change. Recognizing an event might involve comparing a continuous input value against stored data, comparing the values of two or more continuous inputs, counting occurrences of a discrete input (such as a motion pulse), or "timing out" from the occurrence of a discrete input.

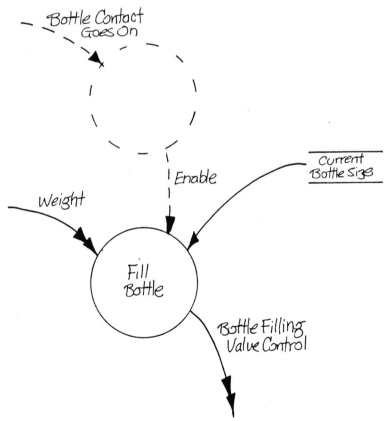

Figure 4.12 A continuous transformation enabled by an event.

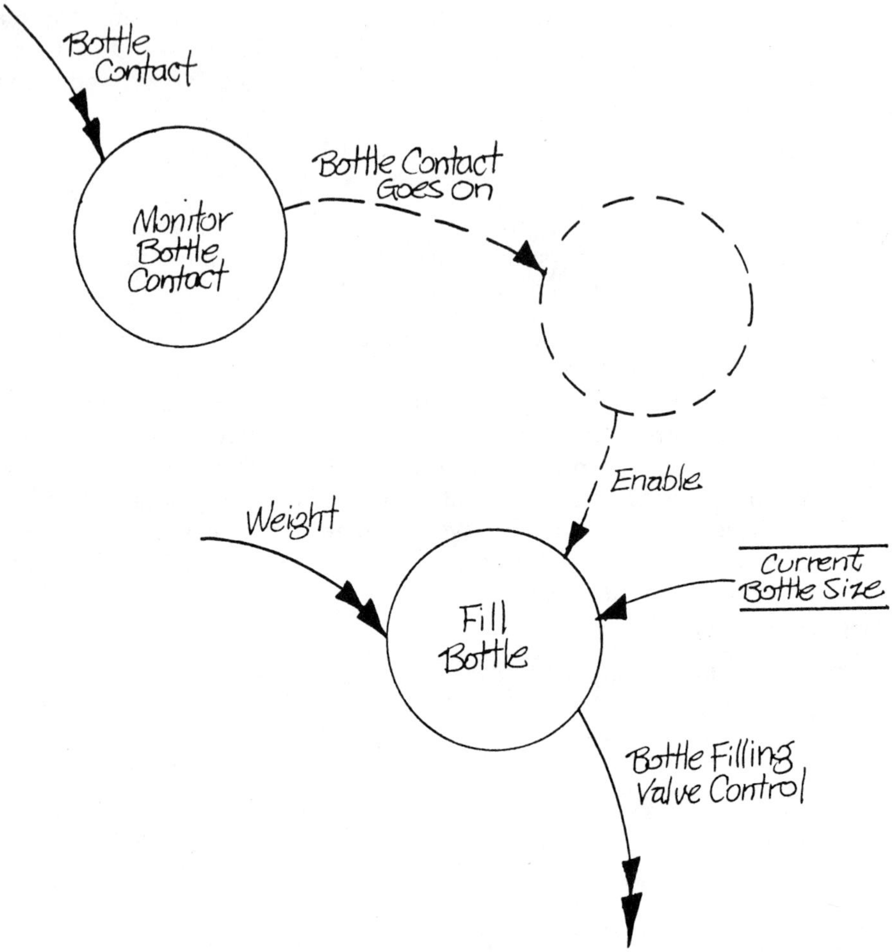

Figure 4.13 An event recognition mechanism.

There are two types of connection possible between data transformations that respond to events; both are illustrated in Figure 4.14. Some event responses need data about the previous operation of other event responses for correct operation. Fill Bottle in Figure 4.14 needs access to the data created by the most recent operation of Change Bottle Size. In addition to the stored data connection, event responses may need to be synchronized via a control transformation. Referring once more to Figure 4.14, Fill Bottle and Change Bottle Size may not operate within the same time interval; the control transformation enables and disables the two data transformations to enforce this constraint.

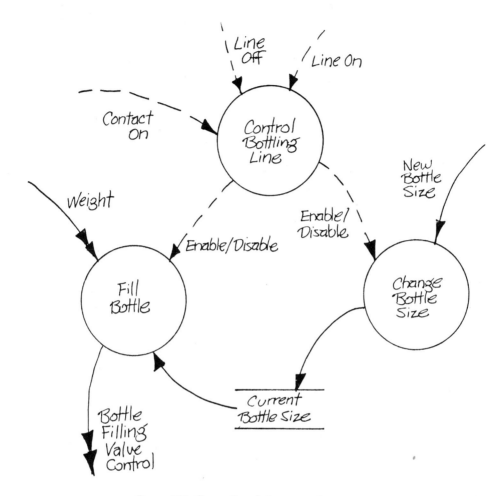

Figure 4.14 Connections between event responses.

4.10 Constructing a data schema from an event list

In Chapter 3 (Modeling External Events), we outlined a method for discovering external events using a preliminary data schema. This procedure may also be reversed — that is, a preliminary data schema may be extracted from an event list.

Chen [1] provides the basics required to turn an event list into an entity-relationship diagram. The idea is to translate sentences describing the system into entity-relationship diagram components by changing nouns into object types and verbs into relationships. (As discussed in Volume 1, Chapter 10 (Modeling Stored Data), the basic structure of natural language is the source for the structure of the entity-relationship diagram.)

Let's take the event list for the Defect Inspection System (Appendix D) as an example. The events Operator Defines Required Product for Production Run and Operator Configures Inspection Surface might reasonably produce Figure 4.15. The verbs have become relationships and the nouns object types.

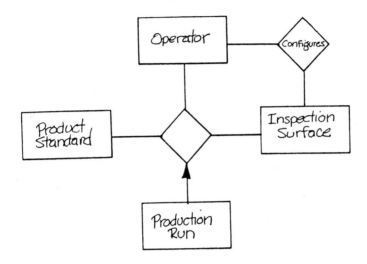

Figure 4.15 Data schema produced from event list.

Our definition of the data schema states that only the data required by a system to support its activities should be represented within the schema. Activities may be carried out in a system's environment that do not need to be recorded within the system's memory. In the example just given, the system may not need to know which operator configured the inspection surface nor which operator defined the production run. If this is the case, Operator as an object type may be removed from the data schema.

4.11 Summary

The information about a system's environment that is incorporated into an event list may be translated into a preliminary model of required system behavior. In this chapter we have introduced an orderly approach to this translation process. In the following chapter, we will discuss the completion of the preliminary model.

Chapter 4: References

1. P.P. Chen. "The Entity-Relationship Model – Toward a Unified View of Data," *ACM Transactions on Database Systems,* Vol 1. No. 1 (March 1976), pp. 9-36

5
Completing the Essential Model
— the Upper Levels

5.1 Introduction

The transformation and data schemas derived from the event list, while accurate representations of system requirements, are often unpresentable. For a reasonably complex system, both models consist of masses of interrelated details with no obvious large-scale organization. To facilitate presentation, the model will be repackaged from a "flat" form to a hierarchical form, using the notation for leveling described in Chapter 12 of Volume 1. In this chapter, we'll concentrate on packaging the transformation schema, from which the data schema organization can be derived.

The leveling considered here is strictly *upward* leveling — the grouping of event responses and associated flows and stores into larger units. The partitioning of single event responses into groups of lower-level transformations will be dealt with in the next chapter. Although most examples will focus on one-level-upward groupings, remember that for a large system several layers of intermediate groupings may be required.

Leveling, of course, imposes an additional type of organization on top of that derived from the event list. The unleveled transformation schema has a "natural" organization in the sense that it springs from the structure of the environment and is subject-matter-driven. It is important that we don't impose undesirable characteristics on the model as a result of the leveling process. We'll therefore introduce two guidelines for grouping the preliminary model into larger units.

The first guideline is that the upper-level groupings, like the event responses, must continue to reflect the structure of the environment in which the system will function. The essential model is intended to serve as a *benchmark* for the designer. Any reorganization required to meet implementation constraints will be evaluated in terms of how much the reorganization distorts the natural structure of the problem. For this reason, the essential model should reflect the structure of the environment at all levels of organization.

The second guideline is that the model should be as easy to understand and verify as possible. The success of a systems development project depends on effective quality control. Quality control, in turn, depends on the specifier's ability to understand what is to be built. A model that is difficult to comprehend will frustrate the quality control process.

Both of the preceding guidelines will assist in preserving the long-term use of the model as a vehicle for specifying *changes* after the system is built. If the model is faithful to the system's subject matter and easy to understand as a specification, it can be used to evaluate potential modifications to the system's functioning.

In the following sections, we will examine a number of heuristics for upward leveling. These were chosen because they tend to create models that meet the guidelines just described. In many cases several heuristics suggest the same choice of upward leveling. When two heuristics point to two different upward groupings, a choice must be made as to which grouping best preserves the desirable characteristics of the model.

5.2 Partitioning to minimize interfaces

This heuristic states that the best grouping of transformations, flows, and stores is the one with the simplest, loosest connections. For this purpose, we consider event flow connections as tighter than stored data connections, since event flow connections require synchronization (see the discussion in Volume 1, Chapter 6, Modeling Transformations). We won't discuss data flows here — a model built using the rules in the previous chapter shouldn't have internal data flow connections.

Minimizing interfaces is important because the understandability of a section of the model is proportional to its independence from other sections. If the reader must frequently refer to other sections of the model to make sense of the one being examined, much of the value of the partitioning is lost.

Consider Figures 5.1 and 5.2, which illustrate two alternatives for upward grouping of the Cruise Control transformation schema (Appendix A). In Figure 5.1, the data transformations dealing with the throttle control loop have been grouped into one upper-level transformation, with the remaining transformations lumped into another grouping. The overall interface complexity of the partitioning is relatively high (15.5 tokens per transformation). In addition, the inter-transformation interface is particularly complex, requiring eight event flows to maintain synchronization.

Figure 5.2 was created from Figure 5.1 by simply moving the Control Cruise Control Engagement transformation into the throttle control loop grouping. This partitioning has a much lower interface complexity (9.5 tokens per transformation) and requires only two event flows for internal synchronization.

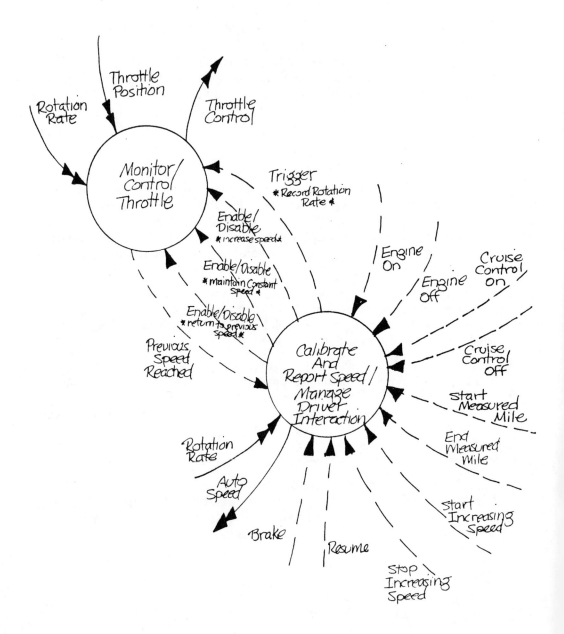

Figure 5.1 Essential process grouping with complex interfaces.

Imagine verifying the operation of the Cruise Control System using the lower levels of each of the two figures in turn. With Figure 5.1, the verifier must continually refer back and forth between the lower levels to see how each of the control loop modes is activated. This cross-referencing is unnecessary with the partitioning of Figure 5.2.

Please note that the control transformations of the original transformation schema may need to be reorganized (by repartitioning their state diagrams) to achieve the best grouping.

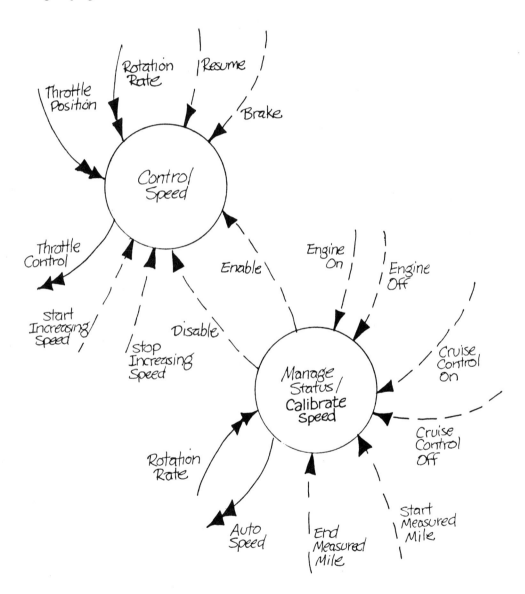

Figure 5.2 Essential process grouping with simple interfaces.

5.3 Identifying hierarchies of control

As we mentioned in Volume 1, Chapter 12 (Organizing the Model), it's possible to use the leveling notation to make a control hierarchy coincide with the levels of the system. Incorporating a control hierarchy into the leveling is useful because it allows grouping together processes that are activated and deactivated all at once. This permits the model reader to understand the details of a group without having to refer continually to the activation/deactivation mechanism.

In Figure 5.3, the partitioning of Figure 5.2 has been modified to separate the levels of control. (The partitioning of the two lowest-level figures is consistent with the two transformations of Figure 5.2.) Notice that the transformations at the Mode Selection Level are relevant only if the engine is on, the transformations on the Manage Control Mode schema are relevant only if the cruise control itself is on, and so on.

Using the idea of a hierarchy of control often requires separating out near-trivial transformations at relatively high levels of the system. This uneven distribution of details is not a disadvantage if it simplifies the overall interpretation of the model.

5.4 Using response-related groupings

Since the basic structure of the essential model is based on stimuli and responses, it is helpful to maintain this perspective when choosing upper-level groupings. For example, if an event recognizer transformation is necessary for the system to identify some event, the recognizer and the response should normally be in the same upper-level grouping.

It's also possible to use the stimulus-response idea in a broader sense. A group of transformations comprising several responses will often coalesce into a single response *if the scope of the system is broadened.* Figure 5.4 shows some transformations from the Bottle-Filling system (Appendix B). Consider the effect of expanding Figure 5.4 to take in the actual bottle-filling and labeling technology. This expansion makes the Release Bottle, Bottle Removed, and related event flows, and the Weight and Bottle Contact data flows, internal to the set of transformations. The expanded schema can now be considered as a single response, which reacts to the availability of a bottle by producing a filled, labeled bottle (Figure 5.5).

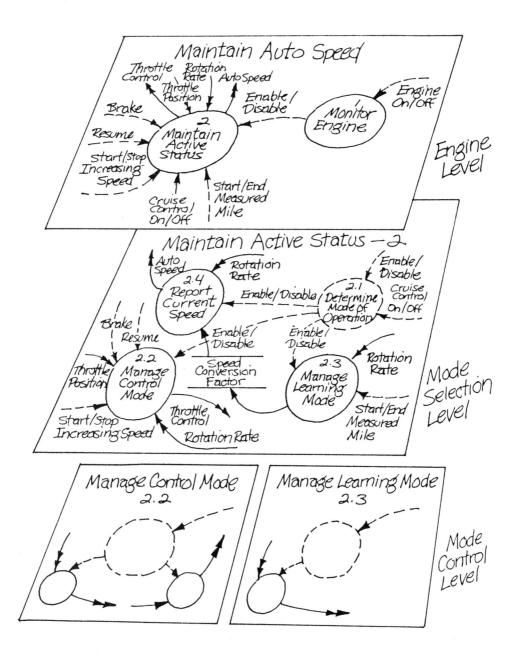

Figure 5.3 Modification of Figure 5.2 to introduce control hierarchy.

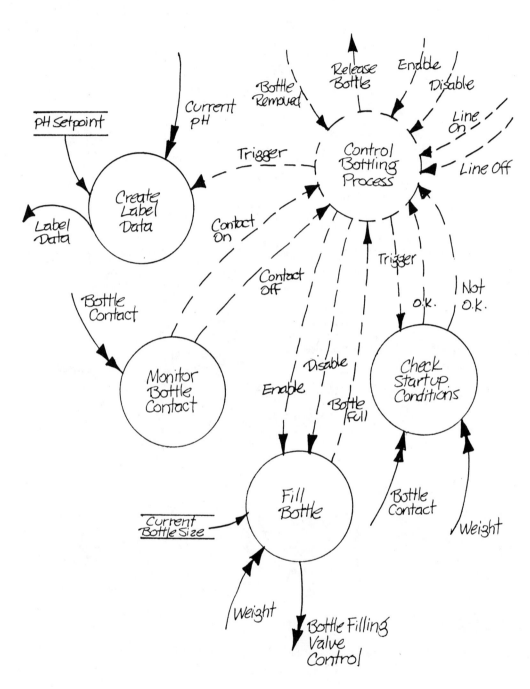

Figure 5.4 Transformations from bottling system.

The group of transformations in Figure 5.4 has a close relationship derived from the system's subject matter, and thus forms a natural upper-level grouping.

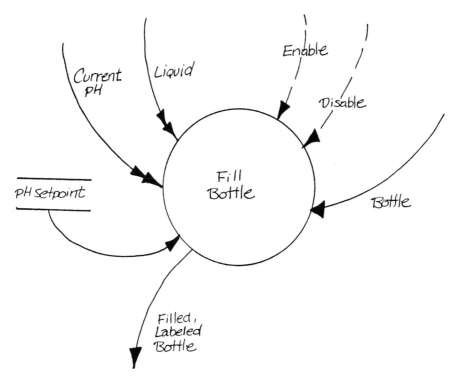

Figure 5.5 Single response for broader scope bottling system.

5.5 Using terminator-related groupings

The terminators on the context diagram provide an obvious source of information about a system's environment. Because of this, it is sometimes helpful to group together transformations whose inputs and outputs connect to a single terminator. Figure 5.6 shows a partitioning of the SILLY system (Appendix C) based on the context schema terminators.

In a system with a large number of terminators, it may be necessary to bundle together related terminators to achieve a reasonable number of upper-level groupings.

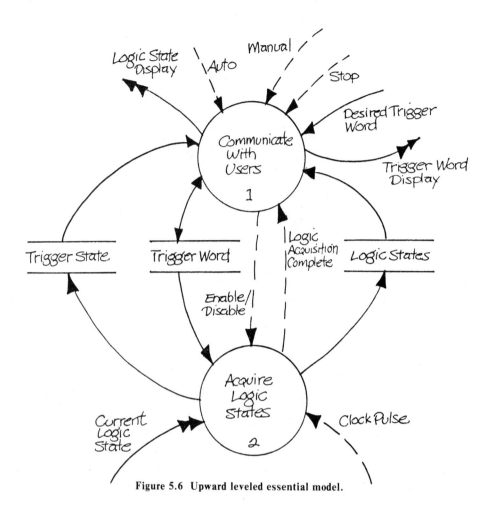

Figure 5.6 Upward leveled essential model.

5.6 Nameability of groupings

A very general criterion for a reasonable upper-level grouping is the ability to assign a subject-matter-specific name. It's almost inevitable that names for upper-level subsystems can't be as specific as those of lower-level transformations. However, if the modeler is forced to choose an unspecific name not related to the system's subject matter, the choice of grouping itself is suspect.

5.7 Summary

In order to create a presentable essential model, it's usually necessary to reorganize the preliminary schema derived from the event list. In this chapter, we have provided some guidelines for choosing the best organization for the upper levels. In the next chapter, we'll look at the requirements for organizing the *lower* levels of the essential model.

6
Completing the Essential Model
— the Lower Levels

6.1 Introduction

In addition to being unpresentable, transformation and data models derived from an event list are typically *incomplete*. Although the overall data and activity patterns are present, the details required for a rigorously complete model are not. In this chapter we will discuss the issues involved in adding the necessary details to finish the model.

Consider the portion of the Defect Inspection System (Appendix D) shown in Figure 6.1. As a result of the derivation process based on the event list, a preliminary model is likely to contain:

- the details of when the Scan Sheet transformation is triggered (i.e., the state diagram for the associated control transformation);

- the contents of the Scanner Data flow (presuming that the details of the scanner have been decided on); and

- the data elements that the Scan Sheet transformation must place in the Sheets store so that other transformations can properly route the sheets.

However, it is likely that the preliminary model will lack the composition of the New Product Standard flow and the (basically equivalent) Product Standards store and the specifications for Scan Sheet and Change Product Standard. There are two important things to look at in this regard. The first is the *structure* of the essential model below the level of event recognizers and responses along with the associated stored data categories. The second is the *source* of the lower-level details required. In subsequent sections of the chapter we will explore in turn the form in which details should be added, and the sources from which details may be derived.

Most issues concerning the form of the essential model are dealt with in *Structured Development for Real Time Systems, Vol. 1.* For example, in Volume 1, Chapter 8 discusses a variety of techniques for drawing up implementation-independent specifications for data transformations. One issue we haven't yet addressed concerns *lower-level transformation schemas* for event responses. If a response is particularly complex, the modeler may not be able to describe it conveniently with a single transformation specification. However, partitioning a transformation into a set of lower-level transformations carries the risk of introducing an implementation bias into the model.

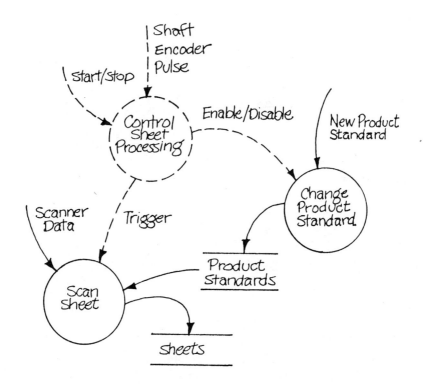

Figure 6.1   Extract from defect inspection system.

In general, a transformation can be partitioned without introducing implementation-dependence if the partitioning makes use of the *structures of the transformed data.* The *data-driven* approach has been elaborated by Jackson [1] in the context of program design. One use of data structure is to expose potential parallelism in the required processing. Parallelism may be indicated when a transformation has a composite input flow whose elements can be operated on independently. Parallelism may also be indicated when a response requires the production of two or more independent output flows. Figure 6.2 illustrates a variation of the Bottle-Filling System (Appendix B) in which violations of the pH control range in the vat must be stored for a periodic report and must also be reported in real time to the Area Supervisor. The partitioning shown is not to be read as a prescription for parallel processing — it is merely a statement that the two transformations are required in any implementation and have no necessary sequence. Of course, the model builder may notice parallelism when the preliminary model is built and incorporate it at that time. However, parallelism is often not identified until the preliminary model is refined.

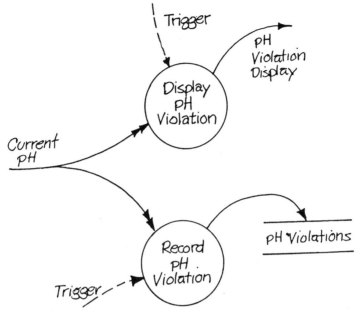

Figure 6.2 Parallel components of an event response.

Another opportunity for partitioning involves a dispersal of the data to be transformed. In this case part of the data exists in storage, and another part arrives to trigger the response. In Figure 6.3, another variation of the Bottle-Filling System allows the Area Supervisor to display the current pH versus its values at recent points in time by entering the desired interval and range for the display. The resultant partitioning is not implementation-dependent; the production of the display requires the extraction of the history data, which in turn requires the input flow. This partitioning depends only on the dispersal of the input data and is a consequence of the basic definition of the system.

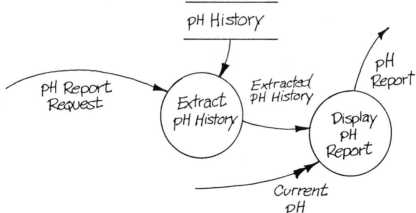

Figure 6.3 Sequential components of an event response.

In contrast to the previous two figures, consider Figure 6.4, which is a partitioning of the Scan Sheet transformation from Figure 6.1. The partitioning involves an intermediate product, Potential Defect Region. It thus restricts the class of potential implementation algorithms to those that perform defect identification in two sequential steps. This is an unnecessary restriction; an algorithm that identifies and evaluates defect regions in one step is a perfectly acceptable implementation and so this partitioning is undesirable.

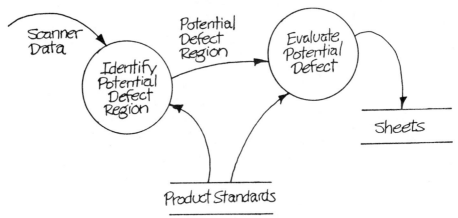

Figure 6.4 Partitioning of scan sheet transformations.

6.2 New development versus redevelopment

So far we have not distinguished between development of a new system and redevelopment of an existing one. Let's now examine the differences.

From a modeling point of view, the major distinction between new development and redevelopment lies in the *source of essential model content.* For a new system (and for the new portions of a redeveloped system) the information about environment and required behavior is typically dispersed and ill-organized. To gather this information, a developer might well study engineering drawings, consult technical reference works, and interview potential end-users and operators. In addition, some of the content of a new system may literally have to be *invented* by the developers, for example by carrying out original research.

If an existing system is to be substantially redeveloped, there is an important additional source of information — some of the new system's content is *embedded in an existing implementation.*

Reusing large portions of an existing system's logic may substantially reduce redevelopment costs. However, unless either the existing implementation technology is to be retained along with the essential logic, or an essential model of the existing system has been built previously, the process of extraction is not straightforward. It is necessary to separate the essential content from the implementation details. If the developers fail to perform the separation carefully, inappropriate implementation details might appear in the new system.

We recommend that an essential model framework, as described in the last few chapters, be created as a preliminary step in both new development and redevelopment. Although we can provide no systematic guidelines for collecting the essential details of a new system, there are some useful heuristics for extracting essential content from an existing system.

6.3 Extracting essential details from an existing implementation

Figure 6.5 shows some details of a hypothetical implementation for the Bottle-Filling System (Appendix B). Let's assume that the system is to be reimplemented, with some changes in the essential details but with some of the details preserved. Let's also assume (as is unfortunately often the case) that the only documentation of current system logic is the code within the digital processors and perhaps some analog circuit diagrams.

A developer might conclude from the careful labeling of Figure 6.5 that the essential logic for controlling pH is found in the Control Loop task within the Process Control Mini. However, the developer is more likely to be faced with a collection of anonymous hardware boxes and assembler-language listings. In these circumstances, an essential model framework of the existing system is invaluable for extracting information.

The single most powerful extraction technique is *tracing event responses.* Let's use Figure 6.5 to trace the system's response to the event pH Moves Out of Limits. The event originates in chemical changes in the liquid in the vat, is transmitted as a change in the value of an analog signal, is converted to digital form, and enters the Process Control Mini. Within the Mini, the digitized pH value is made available to the Control Loop task by the Data Receiving task. The code within the Control Loop task responds to the value change by creating output in digital form, which the Data Transmission task pads with error detection/correction bits and sends as a message packet to a modem. After transmission to another modem, the message packet is stripped of the extra bits by the Data Receiving task within the Operator Console Micro, passed to the Vat Display task, and ultimately appears as a message on the operator's display screen.

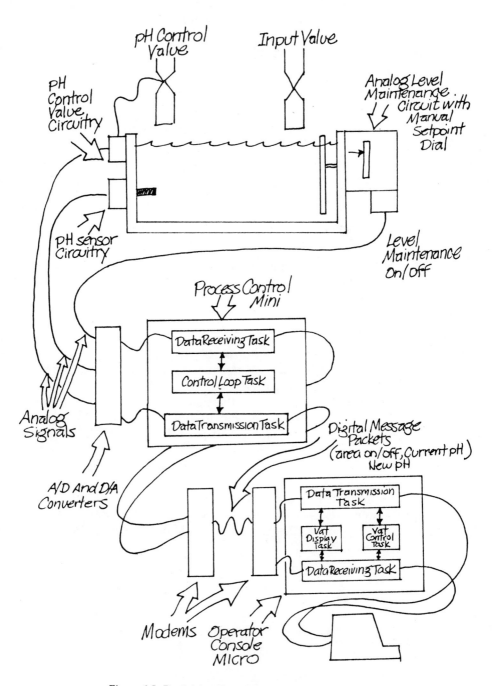

Figure 6.5 Partial implementation for bottling system.

Figure 6.6 shows the portion of the essential model corresponding to the implementation just described. Please note that we are not suggesting that a developer derive the essential model framework (Figure 6.6) from the implementation illustrated in Figure 6.5. The essential model framework can be derived from an understanding of the system's purpose and from some basic details about its environment. Once derived, Figure 6.6 can be used to trace through the maze of implementation details to extract essential content. Suppose, for example, that short-term variations in pH within the vat require that an out-of-limits pH value persist for at least 4 milliseconds before being an "official" out-of-limits condition. The logic to verify this time interval might be buried in the code of the Control Loop task within the Process Control Mini, or it might be inside the Vat Display task in the Operator Console Micro. The 4-millisecond delay is not obviously derivable from a schematic approach to building the essential model. Nevertheless, the essential model framework permits a developer to focus the search for the relevant details in a small portion of the implementation.

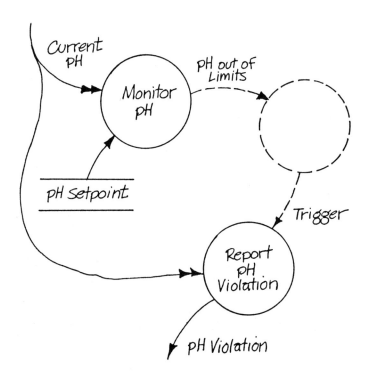

Figure 6.6 Partial essential model for bottling system.

One of the most important issues in tracing through an existing implementation concerns the question, What details may be safely ignored? If a developer understands the distinction between an essential model and an implementation model, this question becomes answerable. Some guidelines:

Ignore data form changes. In addition to being spread across multiple implementation units, a single essential model flow may undergo changes in form that do not change the content of the flow. As shown in the example just given, a pH value may initially be an analog signal, then be converted to digital form, then be passed along a network before it is finally transformed in some essential way. We do not incorporate these changes in the data's form into the essential model.

Ignore implementation technology verification. Checks and edits that arise in response to possible imperfections in the implementation technology need not be transferred to the essential model. A network system that connects processors, for example, will require that the receiver check the data arriving from a sender — in fact, there is a great deal of technical work associated with this task. However, since the essential model is implementation-independent, the imperfections we can expect in the implementation are irrelevant, and they do not appear on the essential model. Note that imperfections in external technology (sensors/actors and the like) must be accounted for by the essential model. The external technology is a part of the environment, and the system's job is to respond to that environment, both when it is behaving itself and when it is not. For this reason, verification of the external technology must be carried out in the essential model for the redeveloped system, as in the example of detecting an out-of-bounds pH condition given earlier in the section.

Ignore internally imposed time delays. Data is stored within the essential model only when required by an externally imposed time delay. In an implementation, data is often buffered before it is passed between implementation units. A change in pH setpoint, for example, may be buffered within the Operator Console Micro in Figure 6.5 before being transmitted to the Process Control Mini. This type of data storage is caused solely by the limitations of the implementation technology; it is not included on the essential model.

Ignore implementation data organization. Implementation considerations can cause us to organize stored data in a manner that does not match the rules we have laid out for data organization in an essential model. An essential data schema can be produced from an implementation data storage scheme by identifying the data elements, removing redundancy, and then assigning each element to the appropriate object type.

6.4 Summary

It is necessary to complete an essential model by filling in content that was not captured by the level of detail of the event model. Such content may have to be invented, or it may be extracted from the details of an existing implementation. This chapter has presented some guidelines concerning which details may be incorporated and in what form, as well as some guidelines for extracting these details from the implementation model.

Chapter 6: References

1.　M. Jackson, *Principles of Program Design.*　London: Academic Press, 1975.

7
Essential Model Traceability

7.1 Introduction

The modeling tools presented in Volume 1 were organized around two major *views* of a system, the transformation view and the data view. This idea is not restricted to models of systems to be developed. It can also be applied at a higher level to the model-building environment itself. In this sense, the current volume has given a transformation view of the building of an essential model. Information about the environment in which a proposed system will operate is transformed into an environmental model. The environmental model, together with further information about the proposed system, is transformed into a behavioral model.

Figure 7.1 shows a common variation of this model-building process in which some of the preliminary information takes the form of a narrative specification document containing statements of requirements. The Narrative Specification Document, Environmental Model, and Behavioral Model are shown as stores since they must be maintained over time and are created by or made accessible to other transformations. For our purposes, the data compositions of the stores should be thought of as:

narrative specification document = {narrative requirements statement}

environmental model = {terminator} + {store} + {flow} + {event}

behavioral model = {transformation} + {flow} + {store}

The approach to model building represented by Figure 7.1 has a major deficiency. Although data is stored about the successive transformation *products* (models) no data is stored about the *linkage* between a product and its predecessors. This does not prevent the models from being built, but it does prevent tracing the connections between successive models after the fact. To correct the problem, the transformations of Figure 7.1 must create stored data showing the connections between elements of the input model and the elements of the output model. However, let's pursue the subject by shifting our point of view and looking at the stored data exclusive of the transformations (Figure 7.2).

The schema of Figure 7.2 deliberately omits the internal connections among the elements of the environmental and behavioral models to emphasize the inter-model connections. It specifies a data base that will permit tracing connections among the narrative specification document, the environmental model, and the behavioral model. Traceability of this kind is in fact required by some development standards (for example, the standards of the U.S. Department of Defense.) Whether or not it is a formal requirement, traceability is vital to effective quality assurance of the systems development process.

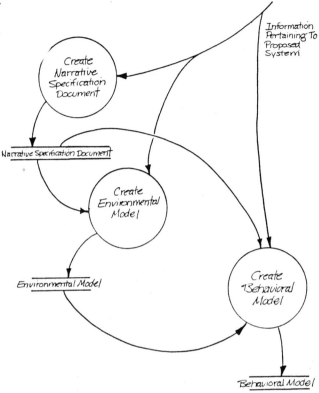

Figure 7.1 Essential model building transformation schema.

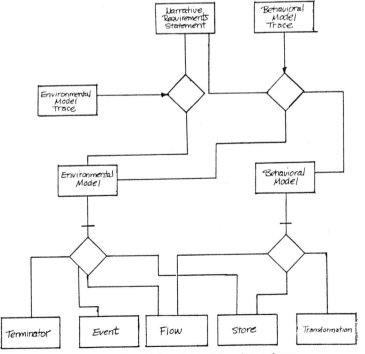

Figure 7.2 Essential model building data schema.

In the remaining sections of the chapter, we will examine traceability between the narrative requirements statement and the components of the essential model, and between the sections of the essential model. Traceability is best implemented by an automated system that is integrated with a computer-readable representation of the essential model. The tracing information could be stored in a database, then sorted and printed in a variety of formats; ad-hoc enquiries could also be supported. However, we will illustrate the basics of establishing traceability by means of simple tables.

7.2 Traceability between narrative requirements and the environmental model.

The elements of the environmental model — events on the external event list and terminators, flows, and stores on the context schema — each have their origin in a need for the proposed system to deal with some aspect of its environment. A simple *tracing table* can be constructed that cross-references these environmental elements to their justification in a narrative requirements document. Table 7.1 shows a portion of a tracing table for the Cruise Control System (Appendix A).

Element Type	Element Name	Source in Requirements Document	Comment
Terminator	Driver	Para. 2 Sent.2 -- "...driver turns the system on..."	
Flow	Cruise Control On	Same as above	
Event	Driver Requests maintenance of...	Same as above	
Event	Driver requests resumption	Para. 3 Sent. 6 -- "driver may ... tell the system to resume..."	
Terminator	Brake pedal	Para. 3 Sent. 4 -- "...senses that the brake pedal has been depressed..."	
Flow	Brake	Same as above	
Event	Brake pedal is depressed	Same as above	
Terminator	Throttle	Para 2. Sent. 5 -- "...control ... to open the throttle ..."	Essential model independent of linkage details
Flow	Throttle Control	Same as above	Same as above

Table 7.1 Environmental model tracing table for cruise control system.

In certain cases the correspondence between the narrative and the model is straightforward and obvious. The identification of "Driver" as a terminator, for example, is motivated by a number of references and only the first reference is included in the table. There are other cases in which the correspondence is not quite so obvious. The terminator associated with the speed control output was chosen to be Throttle rather than Valve, for instance. The choice is motivated by the fact that the valve, suction apparatus, and chain serve as a transmission mechanism for the throttle control signal. The detailed operation of the control loop may be sensitive to quantitative characteristics of the transmission mechanism, such as the delay introduced. However, the essential model as defined here is compatible with many possible linkages to the throttle. This does not mean that the linkage description in the narrative will be ignored, merely that it relates to the implementation rather than to the essential model.

Notice also that the Brake Pedal, rather than the Driver, was chosen as the source of the Brake flow, even though the driver actually manipulates the brake pedal and is in a sense the source of the input. The narrative is quite specific in stating that the system is to respond to the driver's manipulation of the brake pedal rather than directly to the driver. It would be possible to define a system in which the driver directly requested that the current speed be remembered for future reference, but that system would have a different essential model.

Both of the decisions just mentioned — the exclusion of the specifics of the throttle linkage and the tieing of speed maintenance interruption to use of the brake pedal — might be challenged and debated by the writers of the narrative, assuming that the writers are not the essential model builders. The tracing table is serving a very important function if it fosters such challenge and debate, by making visible the thought processes involved in model building and enhancing the effectiveness of the model verification process. Visibility of the thought process is even more important if there are elements of the essential model that are not directly drawn from the narrative but rather are assumed by the model builders to be implied by the narrative. As an example, a careful reading of the background information for the SILLY system (Appendix C) discloses that nowhere is it stated that the collected logic states are to be displayed! The inclusion of an output flow to display the states is an obvious inference. However, it is not strictly impossible that the writers of the narrative intended the states to be stored for later display by some other system, and simply neglected to include that information. The absence of a specific trace from an essential model element to the narrative (indicated by a table entry with "derived" or "inferred" in the source column) is thus an important piece of information and invites close examination by a reviewer.

7.3 Traceability to the behavioral model

The elements of the behavioral model — transformations, flows and stores in addition to those on the context schema, and object types and relationships — may have their origins in the environmental model, the narrative requirements document, or both. Table 7.2 shows a partial tracing table for the Cruise Control System (Appendix A).

Element Type	Element Name	Sources	Comment
Transformation	Maintain Constant Speed (2.2.4)	Narrative: Para.2 Sent.2 -- "the speed ... is maintained." Event: Driver Requests Maintenance of Current Speed	Conditional Response
Transformation	Control Cruise Control Engagement	Narrative: Para. 2 end "driver may tell it to start increasing speed ... stop increasing speed." Para. 3 Sent. 5-6 "brake pedal has been depressed ... tell the system to resume ... " Events: Driver Requests Start of Speed Increase, Driver Requests End of Speed Increase, Brake Pedal is Depressed, Driver Requests Resumption of Speed after Braking	Response to events is sequence-dependent and dependent on enabling -- Start/Stop and Brake/ Resume are only valid sequences
Store	Current Speed	Para 2. Sent. 2 --" ... the speed at that instant is maintained."	needed as setpoint over time

Table 7.2 Partial tracing table for the cruise control system in Appendix A.

In general, the transformations of the behavioral model fall into three types; those that recognize events, those that respond to events, and those that control the interaction among events. A given event may thus be the motivation for:

- a transformation by which the system recognizes that the event has occurred, if the occurrence of the event doesn't correspond directly to the arrival of a discrete input,

- one or more transformations by which the system responds to the event,

- state transitions within a control transformation that permit or prohibit responses to other events, if the event is part of an interdependent group.

(The correspondence between the other elements of the environmental model — context schema flows, stores, and terminators — is part of the structure of the model itself and need not be documented by a trace.)

In addition to being documented, the connections between events and elements of the behavioral model must be justified. The most straightforward justification is that the narrative requirements document describes the event, the nature of the response, the flows and stores used as inputs and outputs by the response, the mechanism by which the system recognizes that the event has occurred (if any), and interactions between this event and others that affect the response. If any of these elements are missing, the tracing document should indicate the rationale for any assumptions made.

The most likely omission in a narrative requirements document is a systematic description of event dependencies. In Table 7.2, for example, the transformation Control Cruise Control Engagement controls the interactions of four events, but only two of the possible sequences are described by the narrative. There is no information on the expected system response to the sequence Brake Pedal is Depressed followed by Driver Requests End of Speed Increase. The "obvious" solution — and the one chosen — is that the second event will not elicit a response. However, what is obvious to the model builder may not be obvious to the narrative specification writer, and it is important that these decisions be documented.

Figure 7.2 traces a behavioral model in which the stored data requirement is quite simple and consists of requirements for storage of a few individual data elements. If the stored data requirement were more complex, tracing between the narrative and the object types and relationships of the stored data model might be more convenient.

7.4 Use of tracing tables in the absence of a narrative

It is possible that a development project may proceed directly with the creation of a model without an initial narrative document. It is also possible that a narrative document take the form of a general charter for the project and contain no detailed requirements from which traces may be made. In this case tracing tables may still serve a valuable purpose. The "source" columns in the various tables, instead of referring to a narrative document, can contain brief descriptions of the reasons for choosing terminators, responses, and the like. Whether or not a narrative requirements document exists, tracing tables provide a valuable "audit trail" of the thought process involved in the model building activity.

7.5 Documentation of omissions from the model

The tracing tables described thus far answer questions of the type "Why was this particular feature incorporated into the model?" However, systems development projects often raise questions about why particular features were *not* incorporated into a model. Omissions from a model may turn out after the fact to be mistakes. This may be due simply to something being forgotten, or to an omission specifically required by the narrative document but for ill-conceived reasons. There is no foolproof method for assuring that nothing has been left out of the model. However, procedures carried out by the model-builders, like the "brainstorming" approach to identifying events described in Chapter 3, Modeling External Events, may reduce the probability of an error of omission.

The thought process involved in considering a candidate feature for inclusion in a model, and then rejecting it, is important enough to be documented. For example, let's consider the override mechanism for speed maintenance described in the Cruise Control background document in Appendix A. Since pressing the accelerator pedal causes the chain to slacken, the embedded control system need not "know" about the override. The system's manipulation of the valve position in a (vain) attempt to restore the speed has no effect on the throttle. However, there are other possible linkages between the embedded system and the throttle that would cause contention for the throttle between the system and the driver in this situation. The inclusion of some mechanism that would allow the system to recognize the override and discontinue the control action makes the embedded system user in a larger variety of potential implementation environments. Choosing not to define such a mechanism might be a perfectly reasonable requirements-definition choice. However, failing to recognize the consequences of the choice is a defect in the development process.

A tracing table very similar to the ones illustrated earlier in the chapter can be used to document features omitted from the model. Instead of listing model features, the table lists *candidate* features, and describes the source of the decision not to include the features.

7.6 Summary

The essential model building process proceeds by deriving features of the essential model either from background information about the system or from previous features of the model or from both. Documenting this derivation process is an important part of the overall job of systems development. The documentation takes the form of a data base showing connections among the system background and model features, which may be accessed in a variety of ways to answer questions that arise during the development process.

Appendix A — Cruise Control

TABLE OF CONTENTS

Problem Statement

The ordinary household thermostat performs "closed loop control" — given a desired temperature setting, it monitors the actual room temperature and turns the heat on and off to keep actual temperature close to desired temperature. In maintaining a desired speed, the driver of an automobile does something quite similar; he or she monitors the actual speed by watching the speedometer, and depresses or releases the accelerator pedal to keep actual speed close to desired speed. A cruise control system relieves the driver of the responsibility for maintaining speed by taking over the closed loop control. The system described here is an "add-on," which is installed after the automobile is purchased.

The Cruise Control System operates only when the engine is running, and is automatically reset to its "off" status when the engine is started. When the driver turns the system on, the speed at which the car is traveling at that instant is maintained. The system monitors the car's speed by sensing the rate at which the wheels are turning and maintains desired speed by monitoring and controlling the throttle position, as shown by Figure A.BKG. The monitoring is accomplished by a sensor that produces a signal proportional to the throttle's position. The control is exercised by changing the degree of openness of a valve, which in turn controls a suction apparatus that draws on a chain to open the throttle. The throttle closes itself when not being actively controlled. After the system has been turned on, the driver may tell it to "start increasing speed," which causes the system to increase the speed at a fixed rate. When the driver tells the system to "stop increasing speed," it will maintain the speed reached at that point.

Of course, the driver may turn the system off at any time. In addition, the driver can override the system to increase speed simply by depressing the accelerator pedal. As indicated by Figure A.BKG, this causes the chain controlling the throttle to go limp. During the period of greater speed, the system continues to attempt to maintain the speed previously set, and the system will return the car to the previous speed when the driver releases the pedal. If the system is on and senses that the brake pedal has been depressed, it will cease maintaining speed but will not turn off. The driver may subsequently tell the system to resume speed (provided it hasn't been turned off in the interim), whereupon it will return at a fixed rate to the speed it was maintaining before braking and resume maintenance of that speed.

The speedometers on many cars are inaccurate, and so this system incorporates its own speedometer. However, the speedometer must be calibrated when installed on a particular car. Since cars have tires of various sizes, the mileage equivalent of one wheel rotation can vary. The system thus accepts "start measured mile" and "stop measured mile" instructions, and resets its conversion factors to correspond to the number of wheel rotations sensed within the time period of the measured mile. This can only be done with the cruise control in "off" status.

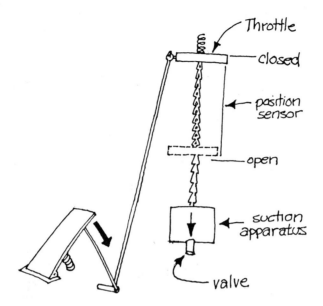

Figure A.BKG Cruise control.

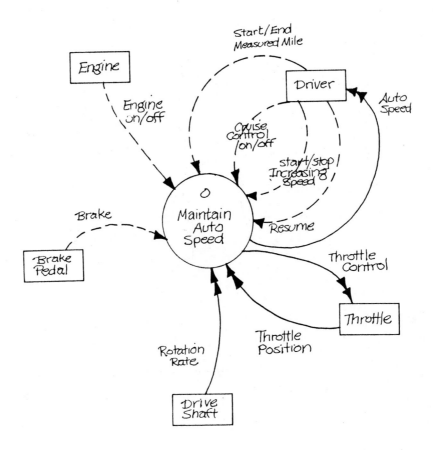

Figure A.CS Context schema.

Event List

Engine starts up.

Engine shuts down.

Driver requests maintenance of current speed.

Driver requests start of speed increase.

Driver requests end of speed increase.

Driver requests termination of speed maintenance.

Driver indicates start of measured mile.

Driver indicates end of measured mile.

Brake pedal is depressed.

Driver requests resumption of maintenance of previous speed after braking.

Speed reaches previous value after braking.

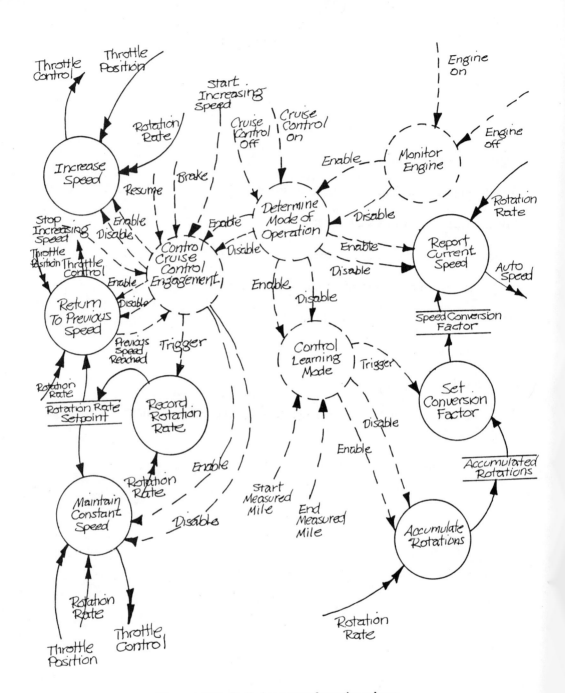

Figure A.PTS Preliminary transformation schema.

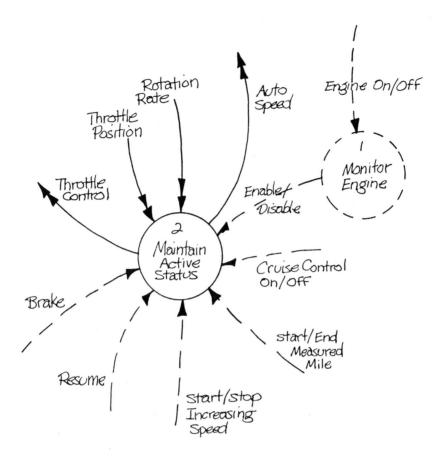

Figure A.0 Maintain auto speed.

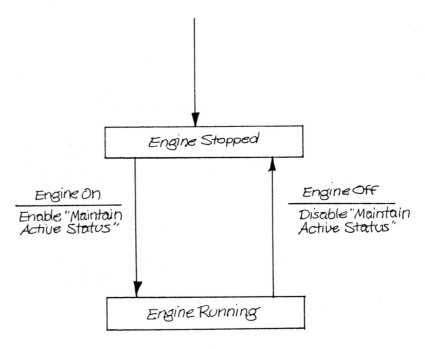

Figure A.1 Monitor engine.

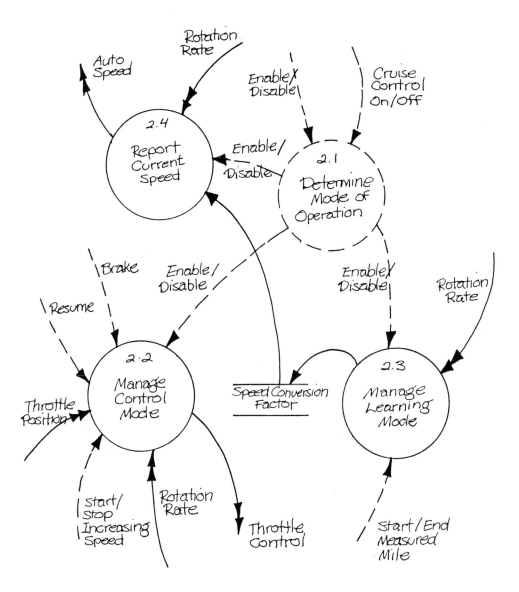

Figure A.2 Maintain active status.

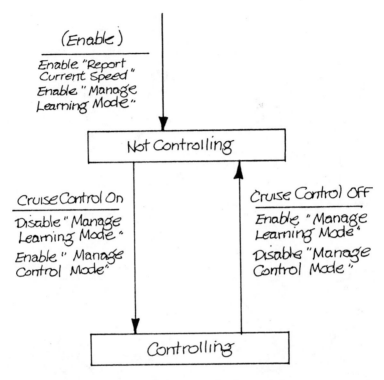

Figure A.2.1 Determine mode of operation.

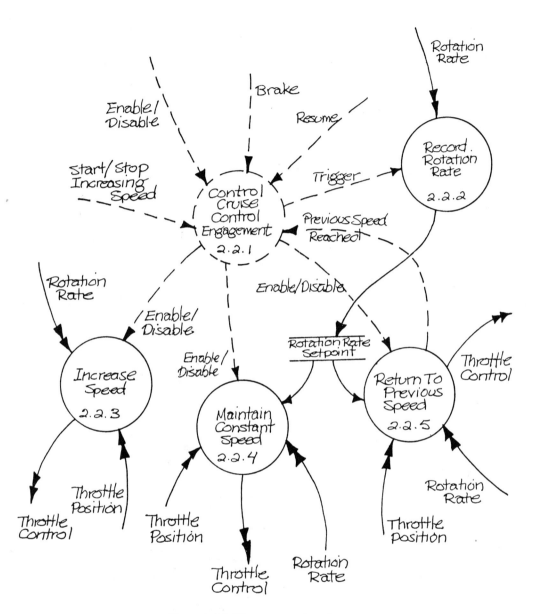

Figure A.2.2 Manage control mode.

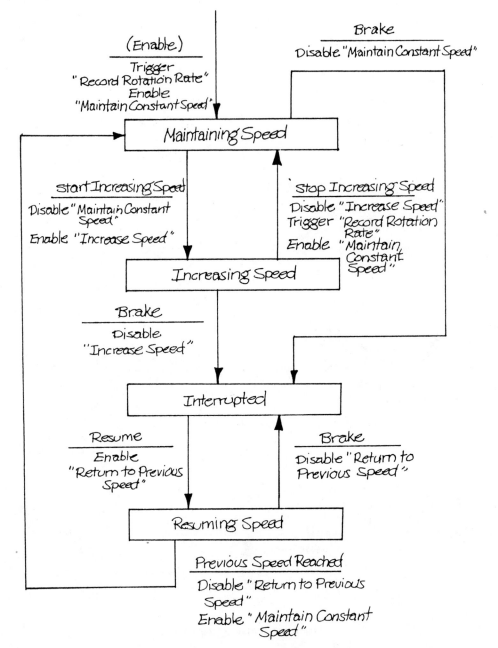

Figure A.2.2.1 Control cruise control engagement.

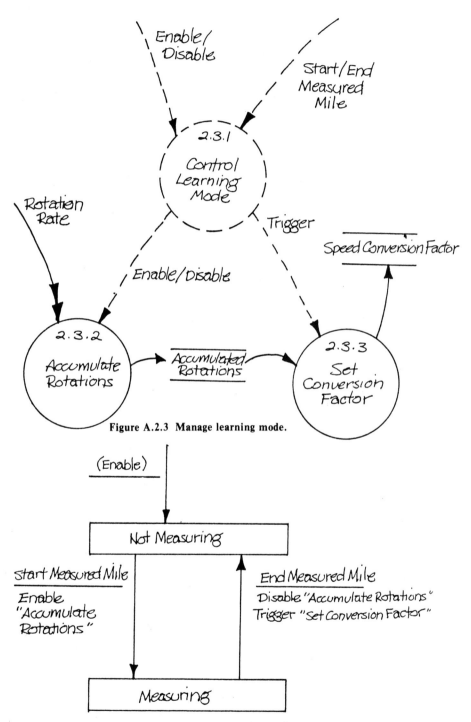

Figure A.2.3 Manage learning mode.

Figure A.2.3.1 Control learning mode.

Data Dictionary

accumulated rotations   =   *instantaneous value of number of rotations since start of measured mile*

units : rotations

auto speed   =   *displayed value of current speed*

units : miles per hour

brake   =   *signal that driver has depressed brake pedal*

cruise control off   =   **

cruise control on   =   **

end measured mile   =   **

engine off   =   **

engine on   =   **

previous speed reached   =   **

resume   =   *signal that driver wishes to resume previously set speed*

rotation rate   =   *instantaneous rate of rotation of wheel*

units : revolutions per second

rotation rate setpoint   =   *desired rate of rotation of wheels*

units : revolutions per second

speed conversion factor   =   *conversion between rotation rate of wheels and speed of car*

units : rotations per mile

start increasing speed   =   **

start measured mile   =   **

stop increasing speed   =   **

throttle control   =   **

                                         units : % of max

throttle position   =   *instantaneous setting of throttle*

                                         units : % of max

Transformation Specifications

2.2.2 Record Rotation Rate

Precondition 1

None

Postcondition 1

Post ROTATION RATE in ROTATION RATE SETPOINT

2.2.3 Increase Speed

Precondition 1

None

Postcondition 1

THROTTLE POSITION at < 80% of max. — Instantaneous rate of increase per second of ROTATION RATE maintained at 2% ± .25% of current value of ROTATION RATE

For THROTTLE POSITION at ≥ 80% of max. — Instantaneous rate of increase per second of ROTATION RATE maintained at 0.

2.2.4 Maintain Constant Speed

Precondition 1

ROTATION RATE within 1% of ROTATION RATE SETPOINT

Postcondition 1

For time ≤ 0.5 seconds after enable, match THROTTLE CONTROL to THROTTLE POSITION

For time > 0.5 seconds after enable, maintain ROTATION RATE within 1% of ROTATION RATE SETPOINT

2.2.5 Return to Previous Speed

Precondition 1

None

Postcondition 1

For time ≤ 0.5 seconds after enable, match
THROTTLE CONTROL to THROTTLE POSITION

For time > 0.5 seconds after enable,
maintain rate of increase per second of ROTATION RATE at 0.1* (ROTATION
RATE SETPOINT — ROTATION RATE)

2.3.2 Accumulate Rotations

Precondition 1

ACCUMULATED ROTATIONS = 0

Postcondition 1

$$\text{ACCUMULATED ROTATIONS} = \int_{0}^{T} \text{Rotation Rate } dt$$

2.3.3 Set Conversion Factor

Precondition 1

None

Postcondition 1

SPEED CONVERSION FACTOR = ACCUMULATED ROTATIONS

2.4 Report Current Speed

Precondition 1

None

Postcondition 1

AUTO SPEED = ROTATION RATE/(SPEED CONVERSION FACTOR * 3600)

Appendix B — Bottle-Filling System

TABLE OF CONTENTS

Problem Statement

This system consists of a number of bottle-filling lines fed by a single vat containing the liquid to be bottled. Figure B.BKG shows some details of the vat apparatus and of a representative bottling line.

Because of the single vat, the composition of the liquid being placed in the bottles is identical for all lines at a given time. However, the bottle *size* may differ from line to line. For example, one bottling line might be filling one-liter bottles and another line might be filling five-liter bottles at 7:30 a.m., but both lines would be using liquid maintained at a constant pH, say 6.52.

The tasks of the control system are to control the level and the pH of the liquid in the vat, to manage the movement and filling of bottles on the various lines, and to exchange information with human operators working the individual lines and with an area supervisor monitoring the entire system.

The vat level control is accomplished by monitoring the level with a sensor and adjusting a liquid input valve accordingly. The requirement for controlling pH arises because the liquid to be bottled reacts with its surroundings, causing the pH to "creep" over time. A constant pH is maintained by introducing, through a control valve, small quantities of a chemical that reverses the pH "creep." The addition rate of the pH-changing chemical depends both on the current pH in the vat (measured by a pH sensor) and on the rate of flow of liquid through the tank (measured by the liquid input valve control).

Bottles to be filled on a particular line are drawn one by one from a supply of bottles, as follows:

- A bottle is released from a gate and drops down a chute onto a scale platform, at the same time depressing a bottle contact sensor.

- The bottle-filling valve is opened, and a measured amount of liquid is let into the bottle. (The scale platform measures the weight of the bottle plus its contents, and is used to determine when the bottle is full and to shut off the valve).

- The filled bottle is labeled to show the actual pH when filled, and the nominal pH. The line operator caps and removes the filled bottle, and signals the system that the bottle has been removed. Removing the bottle releases the bottle contact sensor, removes the weight on the scale and allows the next bottle to be released from the gate.

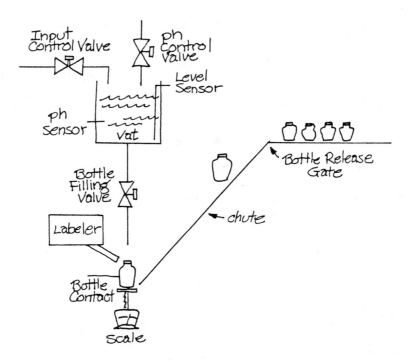

Figure B.BKG Equipment configuration.

The line operators can signal the system to start and stop individual lines, and the supervisor can signal the system to enable or disable overall operation of the set of lines. For a line to start operation from stopped status, both the area enable and line start signals are necessary; in addition, the bottle contact must be off and the scale platform reading must be less than 0.1 gram. The line operators are given displays of the line status (on/off and current bottle size) and are able to change bottle size for the line. The area supervisor is given a display of the current status of the system pH and vat levels and statuses of the individual lines, and is able to change the pH of the bottled liquid by entering a new pH to be maintained.

If, during operation of the system, the pH goes out of limits (>0.3 from the setpoint) all control actions are suspended. The vat pH is then stabilized manually. When the pH is back within limits, the system restarts automatically.

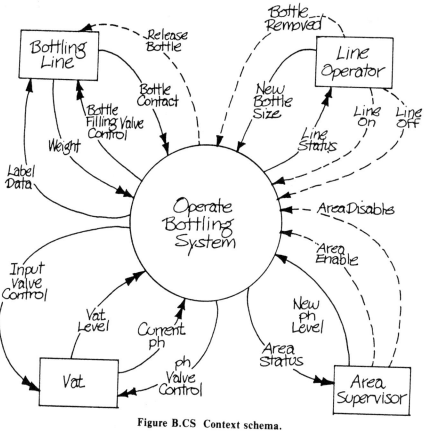

Figure B.CS Context schema.

Event List

Supervisor enables area.

Supervisor disables area.

Supervisor sets new pH level.

Operator turns line on.

Operator turns line off.

Operator sets new bottle size.

Operator removes bottle.

Bottle drops into place.

Bottle becomes full.

pH moves out of limits.

pH moves within limits.

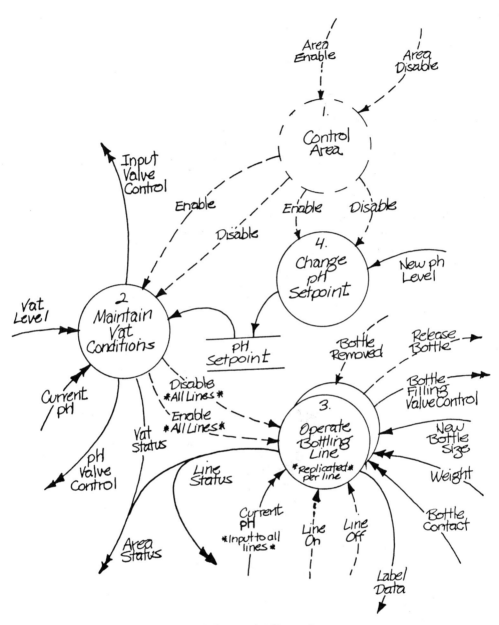

Figure B.0 Operate bottling system.

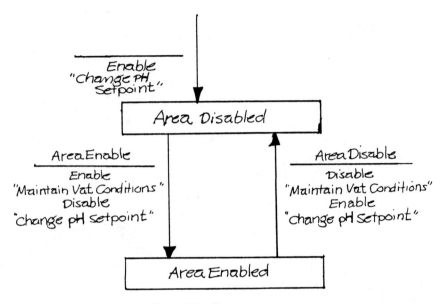

Figure B.1   Control area.

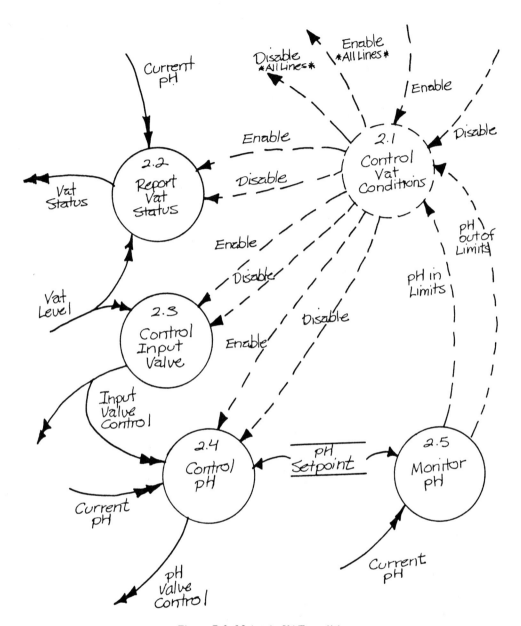

Figure B.2 Maintain VAT conditions.

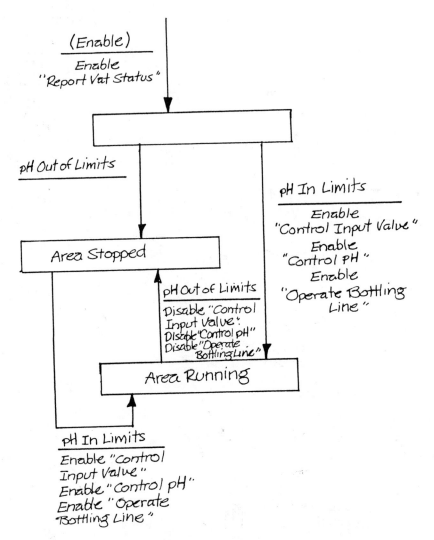

Figure B.2.1 Control VAT conditions.

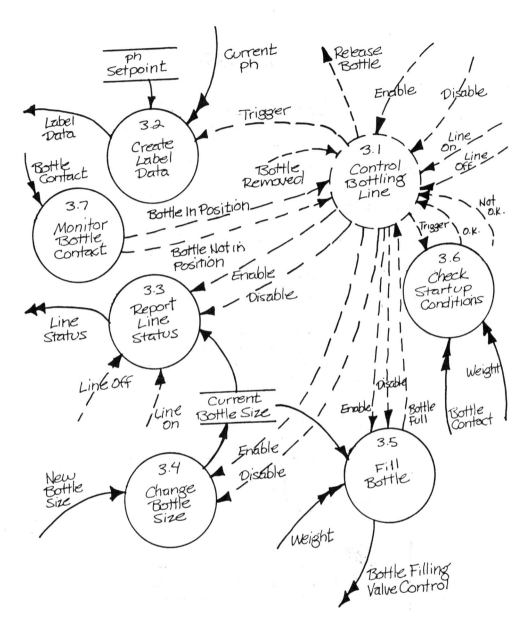

Figure B.3 Operate bottling line.

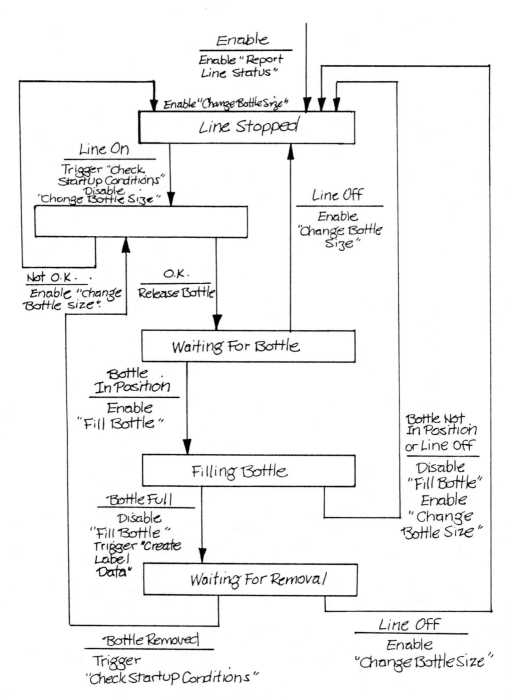

Figure B.3.1 Control bottling line.

Data Dictionary

area-disable	=	**
area-enable	=	**
area-status	=	vat status + { line status }
bottle-contact	=	*signal that bottle is in position to be filled*
		values : [off | on]
bottle-filling-valve-control	=	**
bottle-in-position	=	*units : percent of max * **
bottle-not-in-position	=	**
bottle-removed	=	*signal from operator that filled bottle has been removed*
current-bottle-size	=	**
		units : liters
current-pH	=	*pH of liquid in vat*
		units : pH
input-valve-control	=	*control for valve that lets liquid into vat*
		units : percent of max
label-data	=	current pH + pH setpoint
line-off	=	**
line-on	=	**
line-status	=	line ID + current bottle size + [line is off | line is on]
new-bottle-size	=	**
		units : liters

new-pH-level	=	*change to pH setpoint*
		units : in pH
pH-setpoint	=	*pH value to be maintained in vat*
		units: pH
pH-valve-control	=	*control for that admits pH-changing chemical into vat*
		units : percent of max
release-bottle	=	*signal to release bottle from gate*
vat-level	=	**
vat-status	=	current pH + vat level
weight	=	*amount of weight registering on bottle-filling scale*

Transformation Specifications

2.2 Report Vat Status

Precondition 1

> none

Postcondition 1

> VAT STATUS

2.3 Control Input Valve

Precondition 1 (T=O)

> 0.83 < VAT LEVEL < 0.87

Postcondition 1 (T > 0)

> 0.83 < VAT LEVEL < 0.87

Precondition 2 (T=O)

> VAT LEVEL ≤ 0.83 or ≥ 0.87

Postcondition 2 (T > O)

> control action not defined

2.4 Control pH

Precondition 1 (T=O)

> | CURRENT PH — PH SETPOINT | < 0.3

Postcondition 1 (T > O)

> | CURRENT PH — PH SETPOINT | <0.3

Precondition 2 (T = O)

> | CURRENT PH — PH SETPOINT | ≥ 0.3

Postcondition 2 (T > O)

> control action not defined

assumption: pH VALVE CONTROL = f(CURRENT pH, INPUT VALVE CONTROL)

2.5 Monitor pH

Continuously

> If CURRENT PH crosses from < (PH SETPOINT - 0.3) to >
> (PH SETPOINT - 0.3) or from > (PH SETPOINT + 0.3)
> to < (PH SETPOINT + 0.3) then
>> issue PH IN LIMITS

> If CURRENT PH crosses from > (PH SETPOINT - 0.3) to <
> (PH SETPOINT - 0.3) or from < (PH SETPOINT + 0.3)
> to > (PH SETPOINT + 0.3) then
>> issue PH OUT OF LIMITS

3.2 Create Label Data

Precondition 1

> none

Postcondition 1

> LABEL DATA

3.3 Report Line Status

Continuously

> LINE STATUS set to LINE IS ON if most recent signal received
> was LINE ON

> LINE STATUS set to LINE IS OFF otherwise

3.4 Change Bottle Size

Precondition 1

> NEW BOTTLE SIZE

Postcondition 1

> CURRENT BOTTLE SIZE = NEW BOTTLE SIZE

3.5 Fill Bottle

Local term: FULL WEIGHT is WEIGHT WHEN FULL corresponding to CURRENT BOTTLE SIZE from table (to be provided later)

Precondition 1 (T=O)

> WEIGHT < FULL WEIGHT

Postcondition 1 (T > O)

> 0.999 * FULL WEIGHT < WEIGHT < 1.001 * FULL WEIGHT and bottle-filling valve closed in minimum possible time

3.6 Check Startup Conditions

Precondition 1

> Weight ≤ 0.19 and BOTTLE CONTACT = OFF

Postcondition 1

> OK

Precondition 2

> WEIGHT > 0.19 or BOTTLE CONTACT = ON

Postcondition 2

> NOT OK

3.7 Monitor Bottle Contact (Continuous operation)

Precondition 1

BOTTLE CONTACT changes from OFF to ON

Postcondition 1

BOTTLE IN POSITION

Precondition 2

BOTTLE CONTACT changes from ON to OFF

Postcondition 2

BOTTLE NOT IN POSITION

Appendix C — SILLY

(Science and Industry Little Logic Yzer*)

TABLE OF CONTENTS

Original author: John Shuttleworth, N.V. Philips

Problem Statement

1. Introduction

This project (code name: SILLY) consists of the development of detailed hardware and software descriptions for a pocket-sized logic analyzer.

2. Background

The marketing people, conducting their regular statistical analysis, noticed among their customers a remarkably high incidence of squashed thumbs, bruised toes, scraped shins, and similar wounds indicating the irresponsible carrying (and thus dropping) of cumbersome weighty objects. As the current instrumentation being offered (the Mammoth Yzer), although otherwise creme de la creme, had a distinct tendency toward the cumbersome and weighty end of the scale, marketing felt that here was an opportunity not to be missed and began to react in an agitated manner which, to a casual observer, was difficult to distinguish from hysteria.

Responding at once to marketing panic, as good engineers always do, the designers produced, in record time, the proposed external configuration for a pocket logic analyzer. It looks like Figure C.BKG.

Some of the hardware engineers immediately began arguing about the details of the functioning of the keyboard while others began feverishly writing up orders for component parts.

In the midst of this furor, one of the junior engineers began making annoying and bizarre statements such as "Why haven't the software people been consulted?" and "Has anyone actually determined exactly what this thing is supposed to do?" Finally, in a spirit of good-natured tolerance (i.e., to shut the fellow up), the engineering group decided to take an organized approach to the development and write down some things about SILLY.

3. Functional Specifiation

The thing is designed to be hooked to the output leads (8 bits wide) and the clock lead of a microprocessor, and to collect data (i.e., to read off what's on the leads) at each clock pulse, up to a frequency of one megahertz. The point of this is not just to collect any old data, but to record the states (that is, the output lead values) surrounding (specifically, 127 before and 128 after) the occurence of a "trigger state" or "trigger word." For example, if the trigger state was ?1??0???, the SILLY would come to a screeching halt exactly 128 states after the first occurrence of a 1 on lead 1 and a 0 on lead 4. (This assumes numbering the leads from zero left to right.)

In addition to specifying the trigger word, the user obviously needs some way of starting and stopping the acquisition cycle, and it would be nice to provide an automatic repetition of the acquisition cycle, so the SILLY would restart at some fixed interval (3.5 seconds, to be exact) after the trigger word was found.

Well, there it is. Trouble is, nobody is quite sure if this is complete.

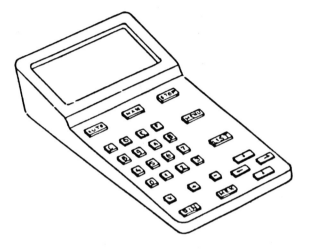

Figure C.BKG SILLY equipment configuration.

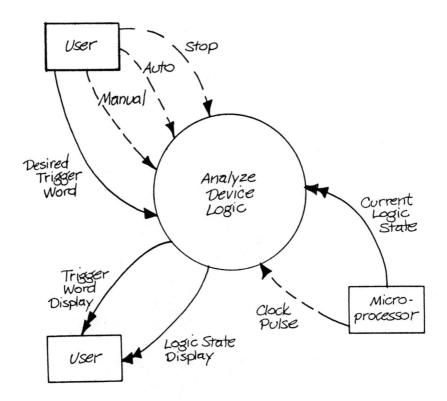

Figure C.CS Context schema.

Event List

User specifies trigger word (Flow Direct).

User starts one-time acquisition (Flow Direct).

User starts repetitive acquisition (Flow Direct).

User stops acquisition (Flow Direct).

Clock pulse occurs in microprocessor with trigger state on output leads (Flow Indirect).

Clock pulse occurs in microprocessor with non-trigger state on output leads (Flow Indirect).

128th clock pulse past trigger state occurs in microprocessor (Flow Indirect).

Time to repeat acquisition of states (Temporal).

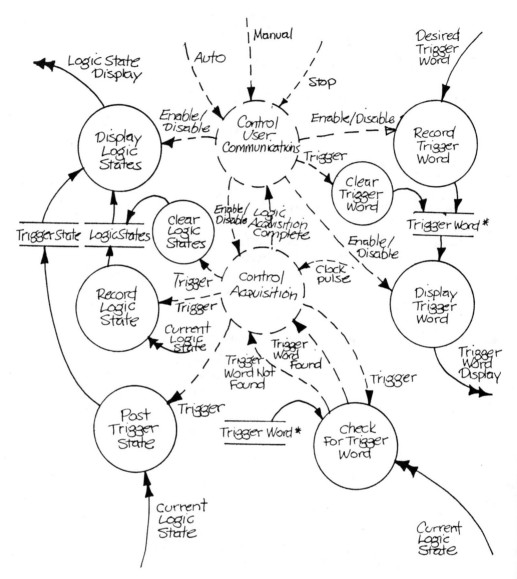

Figure C.PTS Preliminary transformation schema.

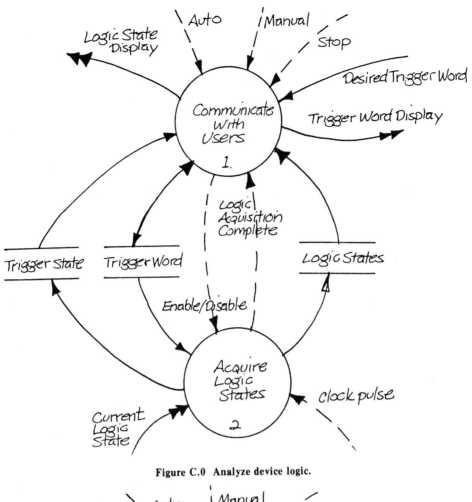

Figure C.0 Analyze device logic.

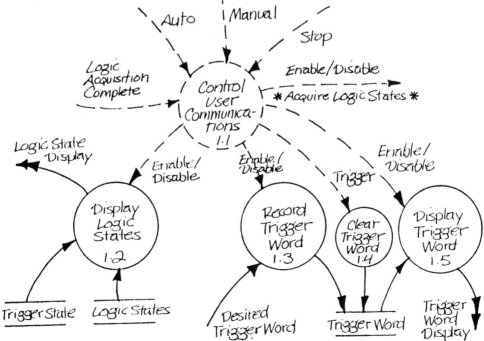

Figure C.1 Communicate with user.

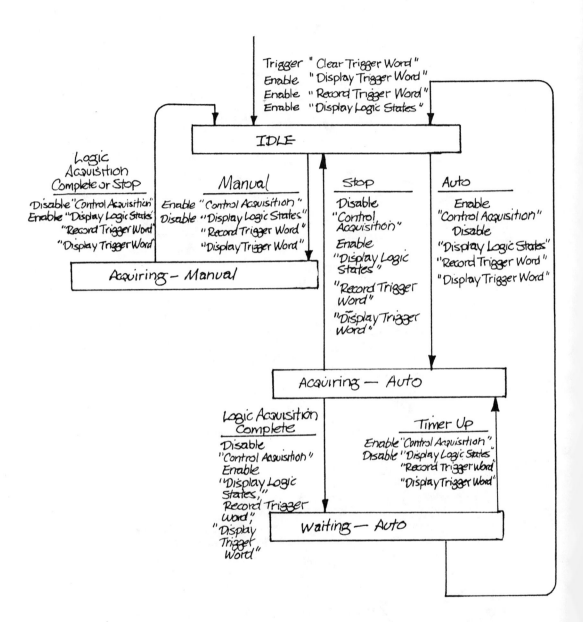

Figure C.1.1 Control user communication.

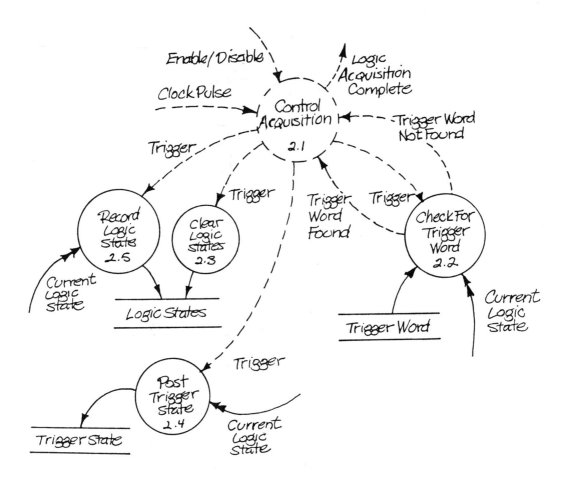

Figure C.2 Acquire logic states.

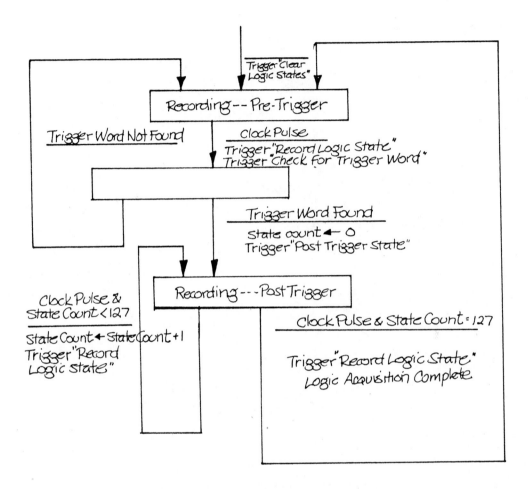

Figure C.2.1 Control acquisition.

Data Dictionary

auto	=	**
channel	=	*the lead number from the micro*
		values : [0 | 1 | 2 | 3 | 4 | 5 | 6 | 7]
clock-pulse	=	*timing signal for acquisition*
current-logic-state	=	*the value on the leads to the microprocessor*
		8{ channel + level }8
desired-trigger-word	=	**
		1{ channel + match-level }8
level	=	**
level	=	*values: [0 | 1]*
logic-acquisition	=	**
logic-state	=	*an acquisition from the leads*
		@state-number + 8{ channel + level }8
logic-state-display	=	**
		{ 8{ channel + level }8 }255
logic-states	=	*the set of values read from the microprocessor*
		{ logic-state }
manual	=	**
match-level	=	*the matching criterion*
		values : [0 | 1 | don't care]

state-number	=	*the sequence number of the acquisition*
		values : positive non-zero integer
stop	=	**
trigger-state	=	*the state number of a logic state that matches the trigger word*
		state-number
trigger-word	=	*a matching criterion for a lead*
		8{ @channel + match-level }8
trigger-word-display	=	**
		trigger word
trigger-word-found	=	*A match has been found*
trigger-word-not-found	=	*A match has not been found*

Transformation Specifications

1.2 Display Logic States

Precondition 1

(TRIGGER STATE is null) or (TRIGGER STATE +128 < highest recorded LOGIC STATE)

Postcondition 1

LOGIC STATE DISPLAY is produced from each LOGIC STATE whose STATE NUMBER is 255 less than the highest STATE NUMBER in LOGIC STATES

Precondition 2

TRIGGER STATE +128 ≥ highest recorded LOGIC STATE

Postcondition 2

LOGIC STATE DISPLAY is produced from those LOGIC STATES for which TRIGGER STATE - 127 ≥ STATE NUMBER ≥ TRIGGER STATE + 128

1.3 Record Trigger Word

Precondition 1

DESIRED TRIGGER WORD appears

Postcondition 1

MATCH LEVEL of TRIGGER WORD equals MATCH LEVEL of DESIRED TRIGGER WORD for each corresponding CHANNEL

1.4 Clear Trigger Word

Precondition 1

None

Postcondition 1

TRIGGER WORD is null

1.5 Display Trigger Word

Precondition 1

   None

Postcondition 1

   TRIGGER WORD DISPLAY is produced from TRIGGER WORD, marking all
   unspecified CHANNEL as "don't care"

2.2 Check for Trigger Word

*Local term:*CHANNEL MATCH is true if the MATCH LEVEL for the CHANNEL is "don't
care," or if the MATCH LEVEL for the CHANNEL is equal to the LEVEL
for the corresponding CHANNEL in CURRENT LOGIC STATE

Precondition 1

   There is at least one CHANNEL that does not have a CHANNEL MATCH

Postcondition 1

   TRIGGER WORD NOT FOUND is produced

Precondition 2

   CHANNEL MATCH is true for each CHANNEL

Postcondition 2

   TRIGGER WORD FOUND is produced

2.3 Clear Logic States

Precondition 1

   None

Postcondition 1

   LOGIC STATES is null

2.4 Post Trigger State

Precondition 1

None

Postcondition 1

TRIGGER STATE contains the highest STATE NUMBER found in LOGIC STATES

2.5 Record Logic State

Precondition 1

LOGIC STATES is not null

Postcondition 1

LOGIC STATES contains LOGIC STATE where the LEVEL for each CHANNEL is the LEVEL from the corresponding CHANNEL in CURRENT LOGIC STATE and where STATE NUMBER is one greater than the highest previously existing STATE NUMBER in LOGIC STATES

Precondition 2

LOGIC STATES is null

Postcondition 2

LOGIC STATES contains a LOGIC STATE where the LEVEL for each CHANNEL is the LEVEL from the corresponding CHANNEL in CURRENT LOGIC STATE and where STATE NUMBER is 1

Appendix D — Defect Inspection System

TABLE OF CONTENTS

Problem Statement

The purpose of the defect inspection system is to chop rolls of metal foil into sheets and to sort the sheets into two bins according to a preselected product standard. Those that meet the standard go into one bin; those that do not go into another.

The system is run by a supervisor and a number of operators. The supervisor is responsible for the overall running of the system including selecting product standards, configuring each of the production surfaces, and selecting sheet sizes.

The four production surfaces are monitored by the operators; presently each operator is responsible for two surfaces. The operators can start and stop a production surface. They also wheel out full bins and replace them with empty ones.

Each production surface is equipped with a scanner, a chopper, and two air jets. Any configuration of this equipment is workable, so long as both air jets follow the chopper. The supervisor tells the system which configuration has been set up on each surface.

The scanner operates by reading the amount of light reflected from the foil. A large percentage of the reflected light for squares scanned by the scanner must be between certain values, as defined by the product standard, for the foil to be deemed "good," otherwise the sheet must be rejected as "bad." Irregularities in the foil will tend to produce values outside the specific range. The scanner returns data for each of the squares by organizing what it "sees" into lanes that run perpendicular to the direction of travel of the foil. Data is produced for each square in the lane, preceded by the lane numbers.

A chopper for each surface can be commanded to drop, thus cutting the roll into sheets. The chopper raises itself automatically once it has chopped the foil. The chopper must be controlled to chop the foil into sheets of constant size for a particular run. The foil may be chopped before it is scanned.

There are two air jets; one pushes the foil to the left, the other to the right. By custom, good foil is always thrown to the right.

The foil is moved along the production surface by a conveyer belt system that can be started and stopped by the operator (to start or stop the production surface is, in fact, to start or stop the conveyer system). A shaft encoder is connected to the drive roll in the belt system; each quarter revolution of the drive roll will produce a pulse from the shaft encoder. The resolution of the system is sufficient to be able to cut sheets to lengths measured in units of shaft encoder pulses.

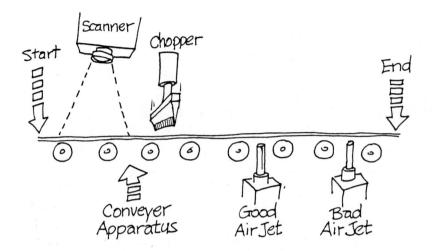

Figure D.BKG   Defect inspection system equipment configuration.

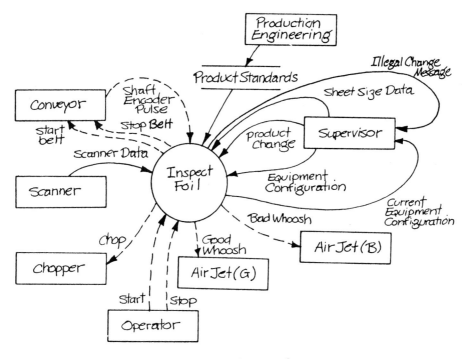

Figure D.CS Context schema.

Event List

Sheet enters system.

Edge of sheet is under scanner.

Edge of sheet is under chopper.

Edge of sheet is under good airjet.

Edge of sheet is under bad airjet.

Supervisor defines product standard for production run.

Supervisor configures inspection surface.

Operator starts system.

Operator stops system.

Supervisor changes sheet size.

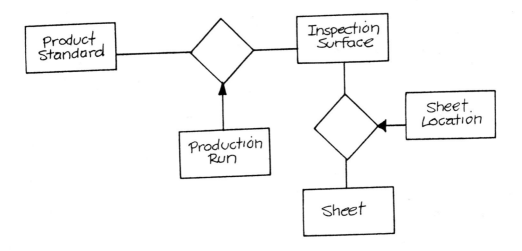

Figure D.ER Entity relationship diagram.

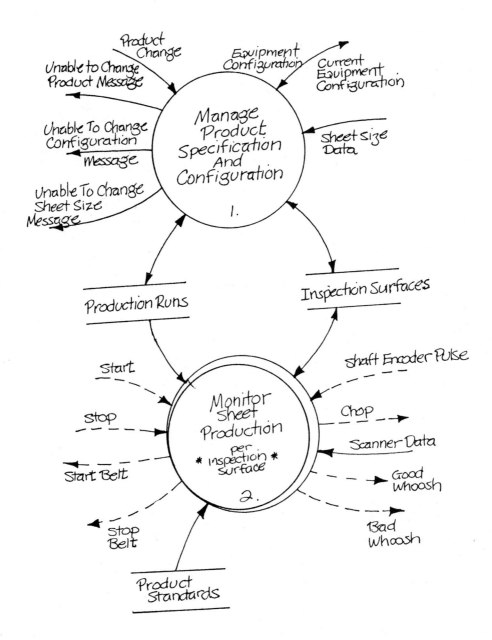

Figure D.0 Inspect foil.

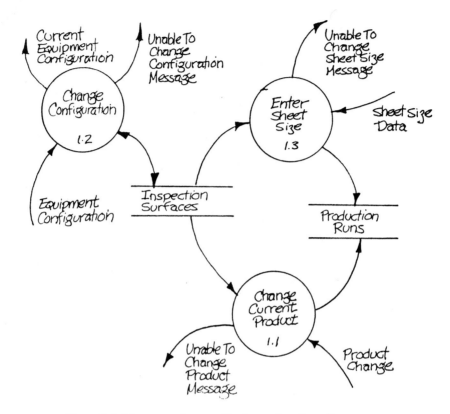

Figure D.1 Manage product specification and configuration.

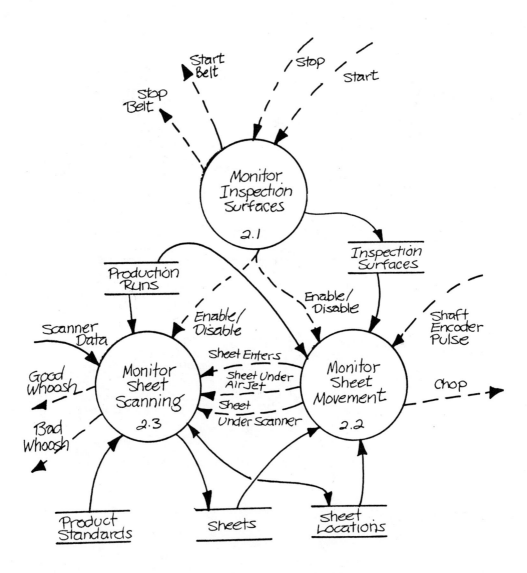

Figure D.2 Monitor sheet production.

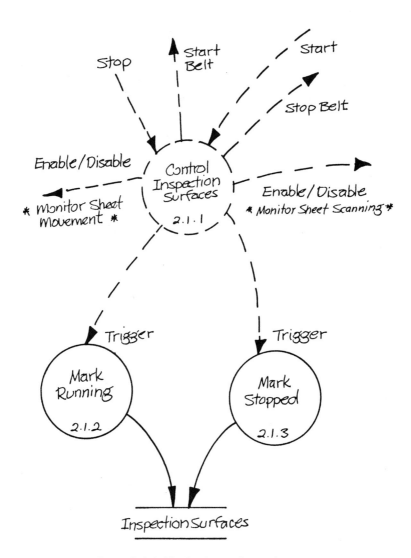

Figure D.2.1 Monitor inspection surface.

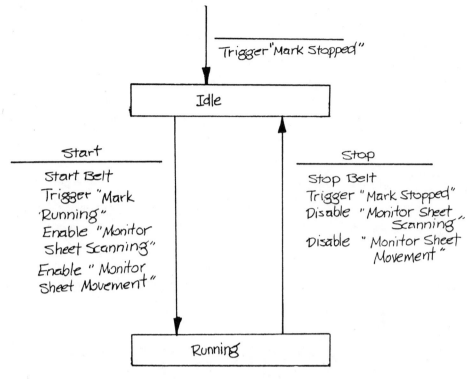

Figure D.2.1.1 Control inspection surfaces.

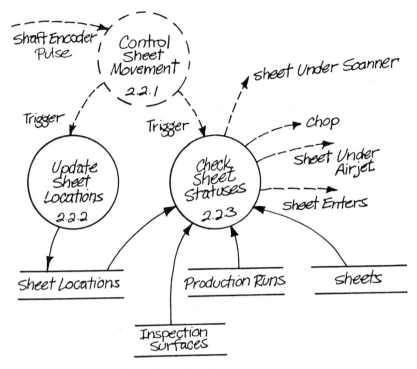

Figure D.2.2 Monitor sheet movement.

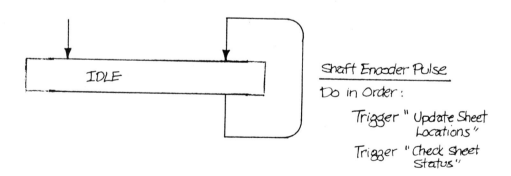

Figure D.2.2.1 Control sheet movement.

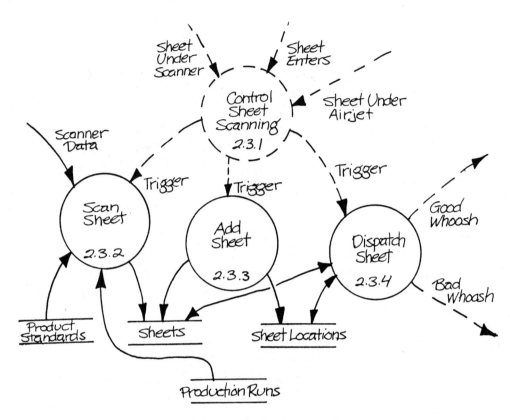

Figure D.2.3 Monitor sheet scanning.

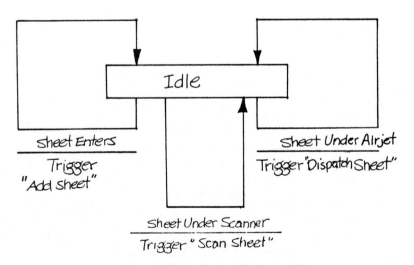

Figure D.2.3.1 Control sheet scanning.

Data Dictionary

bad-whoosh	=	*signal to open valve on bad airjet for fixed interval*
bad-airjet-location	=	**
		values : 1-2048; units : shaft encoder pulses
chop	=	*signal to release the chopper*
chopper-location	=	**
		values : 1-2048; units : shaft encoder pulses
current-equipment -configuration	=	equipment-configuration
equipment-configuration	=	*the arrangement of the equipment on a single inspection surface*
		inspection-surface-number + scanner-location + chopper-location + good-airjet-location + bad-airjet-location
good-airjet-location	=	**
		values : 1-2048; units : shaft encoder pulses
good-whoosh	=	signal to open valve on good airjet for fixed interval
high-limit	=	*high scanner data limit for a given product standard*
		values : 1-1000
illegal-change-message	=	[unable-to-change-sheet size-message| unable-to-change-configuration-message| unable-to-change-product-message]

inspection-surface	=	*definition of equipment configuration for a single inspection surface*
		@inspection-surface-number + scanner-location + chopper-location + good-airjet-location + bad-airjet-location + status
inspection-surfaces	=	**
		{ inspection-surface }
lane-number	=	*relative location of a strip running perpendicular to the length of the inspection surface as viewed by the scanner*
		values : 1-512
location	=	**
		values : 1-2048; units : shaft encoder pulses
low-limit	=	*low scanner data limit for a given product standard*
		values : 1-1000
product-change	=	*the definition of which product is to be run on a given inspection surface*
		inspection-surface-number + product-id
product-id	=	**
production-run	=	*definition of what is to be produced on a single inspection surface*
		@product-standard-ref + @inspection-surface-ref + sheet-size
production-runs	=	**
		{ production-run }

product-standard	=	*definition of acceptable scanner data values*
		@product-id + high-limit + low-limit
product-standards	=	**
		{ product-standard }
scanner-data	=	*scanner data for lane-sector combinations visible to scanner*
		512{ lane-number + 512{ sector-values } 512 }512
scanner-location	=	**
		values : 1-2048; units : shaft encoder pulses
shaft-encoder-pulse	=	*signal that a quarter turn has occurred on the conveyer system wheels*
sheet	=	**
		@sheet-id + defect-status
sheet-enters	=	**
sheet-location	=	**
		@sheet-id + @inspection-surface-ref + location
sheet-locations	=	*the set of locations of all sheets on all surfaces*
		{ sheet-location }
sheets	=	*the set of sheets in the system between entry to an inspection surface and ejection by an airjet*
		{ sheet }
sheet-size	=	**
		values : 1-128; units : shaft encoder pulses

sheet-size-data	=	*the size of a sheet to be cut on a given run*
		inspection-surface-number + sheet-size
sheet-under-airjet	=	[sheet-under-good-airjet]
sheet-under-bad-airjet	=	**
sheet-under-good-airjet	=	**
sheet-under-scanner	=	**
start	=	*signal to start system*
start-belt	=	**
status	=	*status of inspection surface*
		values [on | off]
stop	=	*signal to stop system*
stop-belt	=	**
unable-to-change-configuration-message	=	**
unable-to-change-product-message	=	**
unable-to-change-sheet-size-message	=	**

Transformation Specifications

1.1 Change Current Product

Precondition 1

> PRODUCT CHANGE occurs

and   STATUS of referenced INSPECTION SURFACE is "off"

Postcondition 1

> the PRODUCTION RUN referencing the INSPECTION SURFACE indicated
> by PRODUCT CHANGE contains a reference to the provided
> PRODUCT STANDARD

Precondition 2

> PRODUCT CHANGE occurs

and   STATUS of referenced INSPECTION SURFACE is "on"

Postcondition 2

> UNABLE TO CHANGE PRODUCT MESSAGE is produced

1.2 Change Configuration

Precondition 1

> EQUIPMENT CONFIGURATION occurs

and   STATUS of referenced INSPECTION SURFACE is "off"

and   both SCANNER LOCATION and CHOPPER LOCATION are less than
both GOOD AIR JET LOCATION and BAD AIR JET LOCATIONS

Postcondition 1

> the referenced INSPECTION SURFACE contains the data from
> EQUIPMENT CONFIGURATION

and   CURRENT EQUIPMENT CONFIGURATION corresponds to EQUIPMENT
CONFIGURATION

Precondition 2

> EQUIPMENT CONFIGURATION occurs

and   STATUS of referenced INSPECTION SURFACE is "off"

and   some part of Precondition 1 does not hold

Postcondition 2

> CURRENT EQUIPMENT CONFIGURATION corresponds to referenced
> INSPECTION SURFACE

and   UNABLE TO CHANGE CONFIGURATION MESSAGE occurs

Precondition 3

> EQUIPMENT CONFIGURATION occurs

and   STATUS of referenced INSPECTION SURFACE is "on"

Postcondition 3

> UNABLE TO CHANGE CONFIGURATION MESSAGE occurs

1.3 Enter Sheet Size

Precondition 1

SHEET SIZE DATA occurs

and STATUS of referenced INSPECTION SURFACE is "off"

Postcondition 1

referenced PRODUCTION RUN contains the SHEET
SIZE from SHEET SIZE DATA

Precondition 2

SHEET SIZE DATA occurs

and STATUS or referenced INSPECTION SURFACE is "on"

Postcondition 2

UNABLE TO CHANGE SHEET SIZE MESSAGE occurs

2.1.2 Mark Running

Precondition 1

> none

Postcondition 1

> STATUS of INSPECTION SURFACE is "on"

2.1.3 Mark Stopped

Precondition 1

> none

Postcondition 1

> STATUS of INSPECTION SURFACE is "off"

2.2.2 Update Sheet Locations

Precondition 1

> none

Postcondition 1

> the LOCATION for every SHEET-LOCATION referencing the INSPECTION SURFACE is greater by 1

2.2.3 Check Sheet Statuses

Precondition 1

There is a SHEET whose LOCATION is one SHEET SIZE from the start
of the INSPECTION SURFACE

Postcondition 1

SHEET ENTERS is produced

Precondition 2

There is a SHEET whose LOCATION is equal to the SCANNER LOCATION

Postcondition 2

SHEET UNDER SCANNER is produced

Precondition 3

There is a SHEET whose LOCATION is equal to GOOD AIRJET LOCATION

Postcondition 3

SHEET UNDER GOOD AIRJET is produced

Precondition 4

There is a SHEET whose LOCATION is equal to BAD AIRJET LOCATION

Postcondition 4

SHEET UNDER BAD AIRJET is produced

Precondition 5

There is a SHEET whose LOCATION is equal to CHOPPER LOCATION

Postcondition 5

CHOP is produced

2.3.2 Scan Sheet

Local term: USEFUL DATA is the SECTOR VALUES for each LANE with LANE NUMBER between 1 and SHEET SIZE for the PRODUCTION RUN referenced by the INSPECTION SURFACE

Precondition 1

>   SCANNER DATA occurs for an INSPECTION SURFACE

and   95% of the SECTOR VALUES of USEFUL DATA are between HIGH LIMIT and LOW LIMIT of the PRODUCT STANDARD referenced by the PRODUCTION RUN for the INSPECTION SURFACE

Postcondition 1

>   DEFECT STATUS is "good" for the SHEET whose SHEET LOCATION matches the SCANNER LOCATION for the INSPECTION SURFACE

Precondition 2

>   SCANNER DATA occurs for an INSPECTION SURFACE

and   Precondition 1 does not hold

Postcondition 2

>   DEFECT STATUS is "bad" for the SHEET whose SHEET LOCATION matches the SCANNER LOCATION for the INSPECTION SURFACE

2.3.3 Add Sheet

Precondition 1

>   none

Postcondition 1

>   There is a SHEET whose ID is 1 greater than the previously highest SHEET ID and whose DEFECT STATUS is "unknown"

and   There is a SHEET LOCATION referencing the new SHEET and the INSPECTION SURFACE whose LOCATION is O

2.3.4 Dispatch Sheet

Local term: MATCHING GOOD SHEET is a SHEET whose SHEET LOCATION matches GOOD AIRJET LOCATION and whose DEFECT STATUS is "good"

Local term: MATCHING BAD SHEET is a SHEET whose SHEET LOCATION matches BAD AIRJET LOCATION and whose DEFECT STATUS is "bad"

Precondition 1

> MATCHING GOOD SHEET exists

Postcondition 1

> GOOD WHOOSH is produced

and   the SHEET and SHEET LOCATION referenced by MATCHING GOOD SHEET do not exist

Precondition 2

> MATCHING BAD SHEET exists

Postcondition 2

> BAD WHOOSH is produced

and   the SHEET and SHEET LOCATION referenced by MATCHING BAD SHEET do not exist

INDEX